Simply

Christmas
1994

Simply
Christmas
1994

Great Ideas for a
Noncommercial Holiday

MARY THOMPSON

Walker and Company **New York**

First published in the United States of America in 1994
by Walker Publishing Company, Inc.

Published simultaneously in Canada by
Thomas Allen & Son Canada, Limited, Markham, Ontario

Library of Congress International Standard Serial Number: ISSN 1077-9981
ISBN 0-8027-7441-5

Printed in the United States of America

2   4   6   8   10   9   7   5   3   1

CONTENTS

Contents

'TIS THE SEASON

It's that time of year again. Snow, carols, parties, last-minute shopping, and *The Nutcracker*. Are you doing things differently this year? Making sure you get everything done early so you can spend more time with your children, your friends, or on yourself? Christmas can be the highlight of any year. Certainly its messages of peace and goodwill are the simplest and purest of ideals.

But the meaning of the Christmas season can get lost in the rush of fulfilling seasonal obligations. The presents, the parties, the cards, and the decorations can all take away from the time you would like to take to truly celebrate the season in the way it was meant to be shared with your friends and family. Too often these days, we get caught up in the gift giving and party going and lose sight of the spirit of love and compassion that is at the root of the celebration.

What is Christmas really about? It's based on an event that happened almost 2,000 years ago when a baby was born in a manger, a baby who would grow up to spread hope and love. Christmas, if you remember, originated as the celebration of Christ's birth and was primarily a religious event. But over time, the holiday has become a frenzied rush of shopping, parties, and family obligations. By the time it's all over, you might find yourself wondering, What just happened? You spent three weeks racing around and never even took the time to listen to a Christmas carol, play in the snow, or read " 'Twas the Night Before Christmas" to your kids as you promised.

Of course, it's hard not to get caught up in the commercialism of Christmas. Right after Halloween the lights, the plastic Santas, the fake snow are thrown up on the store windows, and we're bombarded with advertisements about what's the perfect gift to give this year. But is this what Christmas is really about? Isn't it actually a celebration of the spirit of peace and love? What is it that you did last year, or plan to do this year, that reflects that spirit?

This year, as in the past, *Simply Christmas* will give you a number of suggestions for celebrating the season in a simpler, noncommercial manner. This is not to suggest that you forsake all parties and do away with gifts and the Christmas tree. Rather, you'll find in this book ideas that will allow you to spread the message of the season through the parties you throw or the gifts you give.

The Christmas season offers you and your friends a great opportunity to give something back to your community. Working as a group, you can share the Christmas spirit by helping others, whether it be by serving dinner one night at a homeless shelter or by throwing a party to collect food or gifts for families who can't afford to celebrate Christmas.

Another way you can celebrate a "simpler" Christmas is by purchasing items made by or sold to support nonprofit organizations. Throughout the book, you'll find the names of companies and organizations through which you can buy gifts, cards, and other Christmas paraphernalia. The proceeds from these sales will go to assist causes that you or the people on your list support.

When you go about selecting gifts, be sure to give yourself plenty of time. Too many of us get caught up in the last-minute rush to buy presents, when we're more likely to purchase whatever is nearest—or the most expensive. Such gifts may not be what the recipients need or want, and may put credit-card bills out of sight. Remember that the bigger gift isn't necessarily the better one. Be thoughtful, be creative. Christmas is about giving, but giving your time, your talent, or your money to organizations that promote peace and goodwill throughout the year can be a more potent way of celebrating the season.

It can be difficult to keep Christmas spending in check. As we get older, our lists—for cards, for parties, and for presents—get longer. The family expands, our group of friends widens, and our holiday budget grows accordingly. But there are a number of ways to streamline your Christmas budget, which are detailed in the following chapters.

Incorporating the Christmas traditions of your ancestors is another way you can make Christmas simpler.

In other countries around the world, the Christmas season is typically a celebration of family and friends rather than one focused on the exchange of presents. Many of these customs can be easily built into your own Christmas and made the focal point of your celebration.

Don't forget that part of the season is enjoying the many events that happen in your community. Indeed, it seems that Christmas can often bring out the best in a locale. This year, *Simply Christmas* includes a calendar of events that take place in cities across North America at Christmastime. Whether you live in one of these cities or are visiting relatives or friends, take the time to enjoy a little of the local culture to get you in the Christmas spirit.

Christmas need not be complicated. It can be a time of celebration of the year that's passing, of what we have, and what we are able to give to others. Peace and goodwill, celebrated for a three- or four-week period, is not enough. We can use this time as a starting point and spread the Christmas message throughout the year.

Making Your List,
Checking It Twice:
Cards, Trees, and
Decorations

Christmas can be much easier if we take the time to do a little work before the holiday rush begins. Start by sitting down and making a Christmas-card list, a gift list (noting how much you want to spend on each present), and a list of Christmas supplies and decorations you need to buy.

You can start your Christmas shopping as soon as you ring in the new year. Take advantage of all the after-Christmas sales to stock up on discounted cards, wrappings, ornaments, and other extras like napkins, tablecloths, or decorative tins you could use for next year's batches of cookies.

Even if you didn't take advantage of these sales in 1994, keep them in mind for next year. In addition to saving you money, having this done early will free up time for you and your family during the holidays.

For many people, the official start of the Christmas season begins when they make out their Christmas-card list. Sending cards can be an expensive and time-consuming process, so here are a few time- and money-saving ideas.

First, send postcards instead of traditional cards. They're cheaper to mail and can be made by the sender, giving your Christmas salutation a personal touch. Making these can be as simple as getting plain white cards and stamping one side with images of trees or Santas and writing "Happy Holidays" on them. Of course, if you don't have the time or inclination to do this, check out museums, gift shops, or stationery stores for packages of postcards you could send.

You might also want to reduce the size of your list. Sending Christmas cards is a good way to keep in touch with people you don't speak with often, but is it really necessary to send them to people you see on a regular basis? Instead of mailing out lots of cards with just a few words on all of them, send the cards only to the people you see infrequently. Take the time to write them a lengthy note about what you've been doing since you last spoke.

If you're exchanging gifts with someone, let your gift serve as your Christmas greeting. If you're throwing a party, let your invitation double as your Christmas card. You could also send New Year's greetings, waiting until after the Christmas rush when you have more time to write personal notes to the recipients. Or double your post-Christmas thank-you notes as holiday greetings and include a form letter about what your family's been up to during the past year.

Remember, during the Christmas season, every thing you do (ranging from where you buy your cards and gifts to what kind of party you throw) usually can be done in a way that benefits some worthy organization. Many of you are already familiar with UNICEF cards, sold by the United Nations Children's Fund to support its health and educational activities around the world.

A box of ten UNICEF Christmas cards costs between $7.50 and $10.00, and half of the proceeds will go directly to UNICEF programs. You can buy the cards throughout the country at selected retail outlets such as the home-furnishings retailer Pier 1 Imports, which is the biggest distributor of UNICEF cards. UNICEF also sells other Christmas necessities such as wrapping paper and children's toys. So you may be able to do some of your Christmas shopping while ordering your cards. To request a catalog, write to UNICEF, 2515 East Forty-third Street, Chattanooga, TN 37407; call (800) 553-1200; or fax (615) 867-5318. In Canada, write to UNICEF Canada, 443 Mt. Pleasant Road, Toronto, Ontario M4S2LB; call (800) 268-3770; or fax (416) 482-8035.

UNICEF also prints Christmas cards for businesses through its Corporate Card Collection. For information, write to U.S. Committee for UNICEF, Corporate Marketing Department SPBR '94, 333 East Thirty-eighth Street, New York, NY 10016; or call (800) FOR-KIDS. In Canada, contact UNICEF Canada (see above).

There are also a number of other groups whose work you can support by buying their Christmas cards. Purchasing these cards allows you to keep in touch with friends while supporting causes that can make the world a better place.

Amnesty International is an organization that works to free people who've been wrongly imprisoned and to promote human rights around the world. Its Canadian branch sells Christmas cards as well as T-shirts, jewelry, mugs, and other gift items. For a catalog, write to Amnesty International, Suite 900, 130 Slater Street, Ottawa, Ontario K1P 6E2; or call (613) 563-1891.

Museums are also good sources for cards and gifts. The Museum of Modern Art in New York sells boxes of ten cards ranging in price from $10.00 to $14.95. Depending on the number of boxes you order, you may receive a discount. To obtain a catalog, write to the Museum of Modern Art, Mail-Order Department, 11 West Fifty-third Street, New York, NY 10019-5401; or call (800) 447-6662.

A box of ten Christmas cards from the Museum of Fine Arts in Boston ranges in price from about $8 to $12. Discounts are available if you order three or more boxes of a certain type of design. For a catalog, write to the Museum of Fine Arts, P.O. Box 244, Avon, MA 02322-0244; or call (800) 225-5592.

In a rather unusual twist, the Miller Brewing Company also sells Christmas cards. Proceeds from the sale of these cards go to the Thurgood Marshall Scholarship Fund. For more information, call (800) 444-GIVE.

Prophecy Designs sells both printed and braille-embossed greeting cards. A box of eight Christmas cards costs about $9.95. The company also makes large-print cards, which you can send to those who are visually impaired, as well as general notecards, sets of which you could give as gifts or use for your own correspondence.

The cards feature designs by Prophecy's President and CEO Kristina ML Nutting. A percentage of the proceeds from the sale of the cards is donated to support services for blind and visually impaired persons. For more information, write to Prophecy Designs, P.O. Box 84, Round Pond, ME 04564; or call (207) 529-5318.

If you buy cards elsewhere, try to buy those printed on recycled paper. Any way you can cut down on or encourage the recycling of waste during the Christmas season benefits the world you live in.

Perhaps you'll be creating your own Christmas cards. If you have a computer, you can buy software that lets you make professional-looking cards. And if you're lucky enough to have a child who is interested in computers, encourage him or her to help with the design and printing of the cards. As for the Christmas greeting, ask family members to come up with poems or sayings that can be used on the cards. Making your Christmas cards a family project could become one of your own holiday traditions.

Kids love to decorate cards, and here are some simple ways they might try. On one side of a white or colored piece of paper, print a holiday greeting or letter. On the other side have the children paste cutouts of snowflakes, Santas, or trees. Or with glue, outline a Christmas scene and have your children make glitter cards by sprinkling glitter on the outline. Remember that you'll need to save a place on this side for the recipient's address and will have to fold the paper in half or in thirds so it can be mailed. Once the paper is decorated, fold it, staple it, and drop it in the mail.

Another option is to cut out sponges in the shape of snowmen, Santas, Christmas trees, or words. Have the children sponge-paint the figures or words on white postcards or sheets of paper, and write your Christmas greetings on the other side.

Once the Christmas season is over, don't throw out the cards you received. Instead, send them to St. Jude's Ranch for Children, a residence for abused children. (The address is 100 St. Jude Street, Boulder City, NV 89005.) The children at St. Jude's make new cards out of your old ones and sell the cards to support the ranch. A box of ten cards from St. Jude's costs $6.50, including postage and handling. The nonprofit organization asks that orders for cards be placed at least a month before they are needed because all of its cards are sent via bulk mail. Three different types of greeting cards are available: religious, nonreligious, and all-occasion. To place an order, call (702) 293-3131.

In addition to cards, trees and decorations are an important part of the Christmas celebration. When you are putting up your tree and decorations remember to keep four things in mind: Reduce waste, reuse paper, replant trees, and recycle.

Let's start with the Christmas tree. You can use the same tree year after year: Buy a live tree and replant it in your yard after Christmas; then dig out the tree each year and keep it alive by wrapping the root ball in burlap. Or, if you prefer, buy a live tree and donate it to a local park or forest once the Christmas season is over. Before you decide to do this, call your state or local parks and forestry commission to see where the tree could be planted after the holiday. You might also want to check with other organizations like libraries, churches, or schools that might appreciate a new tree as part of their landscaping.

Many states have parks where you can chop down your own tree. This expedition can become a tradition during your family's Christmas celebration. Make a day of it with your children or a group of friends. Call your state forestry office for the names of tree farms where you can cut your own tree.

If you do opt for a cut tree, remember to mulch it once you take it down. (Your local or county recycling office should have information on where this can be done.) Or use the tree for firewood, or as a kind of bird feeder: On the tree, hang some pinecones covered with peanut butter and birdseed for your feathered friends to feed on during the winter months.

When you decorate your tree and home, think about using natural, instead of store-bought, decorations. A walk through the woods can provide you with many things you can use to make your home and tree more festive. Greens can be gathered for the mantle and staircases. Pinecones can be spray-painted silver and gold and hung from your Christmas tree or placed on the mantle or the Christmas table among a bunch of greens. You can also make your own swags or wreaths with the greens you gathered during your walk in the woods.

Use old-fashioned decorations like strings of popcorn or cran-berries to decorate your tree. (Forget tinsel—it's messy and can't be reused or recycled.) Use a length of red or white velvet ribbon, cut it, and tie it into a number of bows to be hung from the branches. Then add white lights and some candy canes, and you have a beautiful tree that can be re-created each year just by buying new candy canes!

Get your children involved in the decorating process. Have them cut out paper snowflakes to be hung from the tree, or decorate walnut shells with Santa faces by gluing on cotton for a beard and adding a little red felt hat. Seashells collected during the summer at the beach can be spray-painted and hung from your tree as ornaments.

Break out your cookie cutters, and have the children trace gingerbread men and stars to cut out and cover with glitter, fingerpaints, or cutouts from magazines. Attach a string through the top of these decorations, and add them to your tree. Gather up any small gift boxes, and have your children wrap them to hang as little presents from your tree.

If you have old screens that are ripped and can no longer be used on your windows, consider cutting them up and using the pieces for decorations. Small cones can be shaped from the screens and covered with greens or construction paper and decorated as mini Christmas trees. You can also form bows from the screen, spray-paint them gold or silver, and hang them from your tree.

Though typically associated with the Easter season, decorated eggs can be used during Christmas as well. Dye eggs red or green, or have your children paint them or decorate them with glitter and bits of ribbon.

Gift wrappings can also be placed in the category of decorations. As with the decorations for your tree and house, these need not be expensive to be effective. Remember, the wrapping will probably be thrown away once the presents are opened! Nevertheless, spending a little time to make gifts look special can make them all the more memorable.

It doesn't take a lot of time or money to make a gift look special; wrapping each present in inexpensive tissue paper, then adding a bow and a sprig of holly or mistletoe is a simple way to make a package more festive. You could also put gifts in the nicer shopping bags you've collected throughout the year. Add a bow and a candy cane, and you've done a bit of recycling on your own. Larger gifts can be placed in brown paper shopping bags tied at the top with a big bow. Extra fabric from sewing projects can also be used as Christmas wrapping.

Once again, get your children involved. Show them how to turn plain paper into custom-made gift wrap that stands out from the crowd. They can use paints, glitter, and/or stickers for their creations. To purchase these supplies, check out stationery stores, dime stores, discount chains, pharmacies, and hardware stores.

A final note on gift wrap: Don't forget that many of the nonprofit organizations mentioned earlier in this chapter sell wrapping paper as well as Christmas cards.

Do you know that you can recycle a lot of the packing used to protect presents? The Association of Foam Packaging Recyclers has information about where you can take different types of packing materials to be recycled. For more information, call (800) 828-2214. Also, many franchises of the alternative mail service Mail Boxes Etc. will accept any Styrofoam packing for recycling.

SPREADING
YULETIDE CHEER:
HELPING OTHERS
AT CHRISTMAS

C hristmas is a time for socializing. Office parties, block parties, and class parties abound. The concentration of social engagements during such a brief period can be exciting and fun. It also presents a fine opportunity for those looking to do something a little different to celebrate the spirit of Christmas.

As you know, there is power in numbers. What can twenty people do that two people can't? Put on a Christmas dinner complete with gifts, for a family that can't afford Christmas. A big group of people can also serve a full dinner shift at a homeless shelter or bring dinners to many, many people who are not capable of leaving their homes.

Rally your friends and family, get them to give their time to others at Christmas rather than buying you or your loved ones gifts. Throw your own party that will help a needy family or a good cause. Include your children and their friends to remind them of the true spirit of Christmas.

There are a number of ways a Christmas get-together can be a catalyst for charitable giving. The following are a few examples of how you, your friends and family, and your coworkers, can bring Christmas cheer to those who are less fortunate.

Have friends over for dinner or drinks, but stipulate on the invitation that they bring a wrapped present for a needy child, with the sex and age of the intended recipient on it. Set a dollar limit on the gift. Donate the presents to a toy drive or to a charitable organization collecting gifts during the holiday season. Check with churches to see if they know of families to whom the gifts could be donated.

You can also give gifts to needy children through the Salvation Army's "Angel Trees." These can be found in malls, post offices, and banks at Christmastime. The trees are decorated with paper angels, each of which bears a child's name, age, sex, size, and a gift suggestion. Ask your guests to pick an angel and buy the present specified, which will be put under the tree and distributed by the Salvation Army. Your local chapter of the Salvation Army can give you more information on this innovative toy drive.

If you would rather give something other than presents, consider holding a mini food drive. This is an especially good idea if you are having an open house

23

with a lot of guests. Ask them to bring canned or pack-aged food to the party. The collection can then be do-nated to schools, churches, or other organizations that are sponsoring food drives during the season.

If you have a close group of friends with whom you typically exchange presents, try something different this year. Put on a Christmas dinner for a family who can't afford to have one. The cost of putting on one of these feasts, split between a group of people, would probably not be any more than buying each other gifts. With a larger group of friends, you could also get gifts for the family's children. You might also want to try this idea out at the office. Put on a dinner for a needy family instead of exchanging Secret Santa gifts among your coworkers. Check with shelters and churches about sponsoring a family at Christmas.

☙ With your children at home for Christmas vacation, this is a good time to focus their energies on spreading the Christmas spirit. If you have teenagers, ask them to get a group of their friends together to shovel snow, run errands, or do chores for some elderly or housebound neighbors. Provide transportation to the sites and afterward have the teens in for hot chocolate, cookies, and a screening of a classic Christmas film.

☙ When getting together with members of your extended family, instead of exchanging gifts, have each person give $20 to a pool. Then throw all the family members' names into a hat, and let the person whose name is chosen donate the money to the charity of his or her choice.

☙ Do you have a group of twelve friends? Celebrate the twelve days of Christmas as follows: Have them over for dinner before the beginning of the Christmas rush, and think up twelve ways you can spread Christmas cheer through a donation of your time or money. For example, one person could serve dinner one night at a homeless shelter, another could read books to nursing-home residents. How about one of you taking an underprivileged child to see a movie or a Christmas show, or buying a book for a library, giving money to a local charity, or giving blood? Once you've come up with twelve ideas, write them down on twelve slips of paper, throw the slips into a hat, and have each person choose one. Carrying out these charitable activities can be your Christmas gifts to one another.

Throw a caroling party. Photocopy a number of carols, and staple them together in a booklet. Then go around your neighborhood or to a local nursing home. Pass out disposable cameras to all so everyone can record the day's—or night's—events.

For your younger children and their friends, hold a "Junior Santa" party. Have the children bring toys that they've outgrown but which are still in good condition. At the party, clean the toys and have the children wrap and label them. These can then be donated to a hospital, orphanage, or a group collecting Christmas gifts for needy children.

Have your friends over for a baking party. Do you know of a church or school that's having a bake sale? Or some group that's selling food at a fair to raise money during the season? Get your friends together for a night of baking and decorating Christmas cookies or bread, and donate the finished goods to the sale.

A party with a book theme can help your local library. Find out what books the library has ordered or is planning to order. Make a list of these books, and assign each of your guests to buy a book or donate the money for the book to the library. Try to match each person's interests with the book that he or she will be responsible for. In addition, invite your guests to bring some of their old books to the party so they can be given to a worthy organization, such as a library, shelter for the homeless, or home for battered women.

Buy a tree for a family who can't afford one, and invite your friends and family over to decorate it with the ornaments they have bought for this occasion. You supply the tinsel and the lights, and have a few members of the group deliver and set up the tree.

There are couple of other ideas you may want to consider as themes for your party—or as traditions you can initiate at your office, in your neighborhood, or among your friends. During the holiday season, participating Lenscrafters outlets will take used eyeglasses, clean them up, and note their prescription. The specs will then be distributed to people in developing countries who need eyeglasses. Put a note up in your office or around your neighborhood, and see if you can get people to donate their old glasses. For more information about the program, call (800) 522-LENS.

Your neighborhood dry cleaner may participate in a "Coats for Kids" program. Through this program, you can donate the coats your children have outgrown. The dry cleaners will clean the coats and give them to a local charity to be distributed to needy children. Ask your dry cleaner if it participates in this program, or check with a local dry cleaners association.

Not all Christmas celebrations need to be centered on doing something for others, but there are little things you can do if you are entertaining that will help out charitable organizations. For example, if you are having a party at your home or office, there's a number you can call to find out where you can donate leftover food to a homeless shelter or a home for battered families. Call Foodchain at (800) 845-3008, Monday through Friday between the hours of 8:30 A.M. and 4:30 P.M. (EST). This organization will be able to direct you to a shelter or organization that could use the food.

From Advent
to Epiphany:
A Calendar
of Days

The Christmas season is rich with traditions handed down through the generations. As each family welcomes new members, new customs are added to the Christmas celebration, giving the season a strong sense of family history and evolution. These little rituals can be the most memorable things you do during the holidays, and may be your children's favorite part of the season, which they will look back on fondly when they are adults.

Because America is a patchwork of cultures, many of our Christmas traditions were adopted from the countries of our ancestors. The Christmas tree originated in Germany and Christmas cards in England. The tradition of having lights in the window comes from Ireland, where during times of religious suppression a Catholic household left lights in the window and the doors unlocked, so that a passing priest would know it was a home where he would be welcome to celebrate Christmas Mass.

Mistletoe has pagan origins. In Scandinavia, it was known as a plant of peace. Legend has it that enemies who met beneath the boughs would lay down their arms and declare a truce. Somehow that evolved into the traditional kiss when a person is caught standing beneath a sprig of the plant.

According to legend, the poinsettia, perhaps the most familiar Christmas plant, was brought to a creche by a Mexican boy who had no other gifts to bring to the baby Jesus. The first creche was created by St. Francis of Assisi in Italy, sometime during the thirteenth century.

For Christians, the celebration of Christmas begins with Advent, a season devoted to preparing for the birth of Christ. Advent begins on the Sunday closest to the feast of St. Andrew, which is November 30, or the fourth Sunday before Christmas. Two popular symbols of the Advent season can be found in many homes: the Advent wreath and the Advent calendar. The Advent wreath was created by Lutherans and is made of three purple candles and a sole pink one nested in a circle of greens. One candle is lit on each of the four Sundays of the season, with the pink candle being lit the third Sunday of Advent.

The Advent calendar originated in Germany. The windows of the calendar, one of which is opened every day, depict scenes anticipating the arrival of Christmas day.

The Christmas season stretches from the first Sunday of Advent to the Feast of the Epiphany, also the last day of the twelve days of Christmas or January 6. In many countries Christmas is celebrated over a number of days, with December 25 being a day of religious observance and the other days being devoted to gift giving or visiting with friends and relatives.

What follows is a calendar of days for the Christmas season for 1994. There are a number of "special" days that can serve as a theme for a party or as a means of teaching your children about the different ways the season is celebrated around the world.

November 27: First Sunday of Advent

December 4: St. Barbara's Day
Tradition has it that if a girl puts a twig from a cherry tree in water, and if it blooms by Christmas Eve, she will be married the following year.

December 5: St. Nicholas Eve
In western Europe, the family shares stories about the life of St. Nicholas. St. Nicholas is the patron saint of children, sailors, Russia,

pilgrims, and, curiously enough, pawnbrokers. Once the bishop of Myra, a city in Asia Minor, St. Nicholas was known for his love of children and for his generosity. Over time, the legend of St. Nicholas evolved into what we now know as Santa Claus. To celebrate this night with your family, you might want to get your children together for a special reading of a Christmas story or for a viewing of one of your favorite Christmas movies like *It's a Wonderful Life* or *Miracle on 34th Street*.

December 6: Feast of St. Nicholas

In many countries in western Europe, children put their shoes outside their doors on St. Nicholas Eve, and when they wake up in the morning, the shoes are filled with candy and presents. You could add a twist to this celebration. Throw a St. Nicholas Eve party, and invite your friends to bring their old shoes, both dress and athletic. The collected goods could then be given to a shelter or an organization that distributes clothing to shelters or to people in disaster areas.

December 12: Poinsettia Day

This day is set aside to enjoy the most recognizable Christmas plant. It was brought to the United States in the mid 1800s by an American statesman named Dr. Joel Poinsett. Poinsett served as a member of the U.S. Congress and as secretary of war.

December 13: St. Lucia Day

This Swedish holiday has both Catholic and pagan origins. Most say that the name is borrowed from the blind martyr St. Lucia. The day marks winter's longest and darkest night. Since the early 1700s, as part of the celebration, a young girl dressed in a white robe and wearing a wreath of lit candles on her head wakes the village or household. She serves coffee and *lussekatter,* a saffron sweet bread, and leads the family or village in singing traditional folk songs.

December 15

In Puerto Rico, this date marks the beginning of Navidades, the official start of the Christmas celebration, which runs through

January 6 of the following year. During the holiday, gifts are given out both on Christmas Day and on Three Kings Day (January 6).

December 16: Posadas Day
This holiday is observed in Mexico and in many Mexican-American communities in the United States. Also known as the "Lodgings," the celebration lasts nine days, until December 24. Since the holiday commemorates the journey of Mary and Joseph to Bethlehem, communities will often stage a procession of the Holy Family on one of the nine days. Religious ceremonies and festivities, such as the well-known breaking of the piñata, all occur during these nine days.

December 24: Christmas Eve
On this night, families traditionally gather for meals and gift giving. Many choose to attend religious services on Christmas Eve rather than on Christmas Day. In Austria, there are "Silent Night, Holy Night" celebrations commemorating the creation of this Christmas carol. In Moscow, the bells of St. Basil's Cathedral in

Red Square are rung on Christmas Eve. After Lenin's death in 1924, this custom was prohibited by the government for decades; it was resumed in 1990.

December 25: Christmas Day

Christmas was not actually celebrated as a special feast until about the middle of the fourth century, when Rome chose this date to celebrate the Nativity of Christ. There is some debate about whether December 25 was actually the birth date of Christ. It is thought that this date was selected so the Christian celebration would overshadow the pagan festival of Saturnalia, which runs from December 17 through December 23. The ancient Roman festival honors Saturn, the planter god, and was one of the most jubilant celebrations of that time.

December 26: Feast of St. Stephen

This is a public holiday in Austria and also observed as Boxing Day in the United Kingdom, with the exception of Scotland. Traditionally, gifts were given to workers on Boxing Day. It is now a national holiday in England, Canada, and Wales. In many countries, December 26 is considered the second day of Christmas and is observed as a holiday.

December 27: Feast of St. John
Scandinavians celebrate this occasion by visiting friends and relatives.

December 28: Holy Innocents Day, or Childermas
This day commemorates the slaughter of children in Bethlehem that was ordered by King Herod, who wished to destroy the baby Jesus.

December 31: New Year's Eve
Typically a night of revelry welcoming the beginning of a new year (according to the Gregorian calendar).

January 1: New Year's Day
In many countries around the world, January 1 is a public holiday. It is often a day of reflection when people make their resolutions for the new year.

January 5
Epiphany Eve, also known as the Twelfth Night (it's the last of the twelve days of Christmas). This night has a history of celebration and mischievousness.

January 6: Feast of the Epiphany, or Three Kings Day
This day commemorates the Star of Bethlehem leading the Magi, or Three Wise Men, to the manger in Bethlehem. It is also observed as Christmas by the Armenian Church.

In Italy, January 6 is La Befana, a festival during which a kind witch gives toys and candy to children who've been good and coal to those who have not.

A few other things you could do to add your own "traditions" to the holidays might include presenting each member of the family with a special ornament recognizing a goal that he or she achieved that year. Your tree then becomes a symbol of everything you and your children accomplish through the years.

You could also keep a special Christmas book each year. Invite family members or holiday guests to write in it. Have them put pictures in it, or draw something in the book that reminds them of the year that's coming to a close. Bring out the old books every year for a walk down memory lane.

Make Christmas last a little longer by letting the children open a big present on Christmas Day and a series of smaller presents on each of the twelve days of Christmas.

On Christmas Eve, have members of the family read their favorite Christmas stories aloud. Or designate Secret Santas so one person is responsible for filling the stocking of another family member. You could also draw names from a hat so each family member buys gifts for only one person instead of every member of the family.

Christmas Festivities

in the

United States

and Canada

I nstead of giving your friends gifts this year, why not get to-gether and take in one of the many exhibitions, plays, or concerts that are presented in your town or a nearby city during the Christmas season? Going to *The Nutcracker,* to the lighting of the town's Christmas tree, or to a choir concert is a great way to get in the Christmas spirit and spend time with family and friends.

Christmas can bring out the best in cities across North America. Not only do these towns look and sound terrific, with all the lights and music, but they also put on some wonderful free shows. So while the family outing won't put a big dent in your pocketbook, it should provide you with some very fond memories.

What follows is a selected list of events that take place at Christmastime in a number of North American cities. Events that are included would be good outings for families and are either free or inexpensive.

You'll notice that some dates for these events aren't included. That's because as of this writing many cities hadn't yet firmed up their plans for the holiday season. But you can call the telephone numbers provided for more information about local events. If your city, or one you'll be visiting during Christmas, isn't on the list, call the city's Chamber of Commerce or Visitors Information Bureau for more information on events planned for the holiday season.

ALBUQUERQUE, NEW MEXICO

Albuquerque Convention and Visitors Bureau, in state (505) 842-9918, out of state (800) 733-9918.
DECEMBER 11: Los Posadas on the West Mesa, a traditional reenactment of Mary and Joseph's search for shelter in Bethlehem; (505) 897-0047.
DECEMBER 24–29: Christmas Indian dances, at pueblos across the state. For more information, call (505) 843-7270.
DECEMBER 24: Luminaria or *farolitos*. Albuquerque is lit up with little candles placed in paper bags, as a way of welcoming Jesus into the world.

ATLANTA, GEORGIA

Atlanta Convention and Visitors Bureau, (404) 222-6688.
NOVEMBER 25: Lighting of the "Great Tree," Underground Atlanta; (404) 523–2311.

NOVEMBER 29–DECEMBER 12: Christmas at Callanwolde, Callanwolde Fine Arts Center; (404) 872-5338.

DECEMBER 4–15: Annual Country Christmas Celebration, Piedmont Park at the Prado; (404) 876-5859.

OTHER EVENTS: Festival of Trees, Georgia World Congress Center; (404) 223-4000.

BOSTON, MASSACHUSETTS

Greater Boston Convention and Visitors Bureau, (617) 536-4100.

DECEMBER 2–3: Festival of Lights Weekend: Twenty-second Annual Prudential Tree Lighting; Second Annual Sleigh Bell Parade; Fifty-fourth Annual Boston Common Tree Lighting/Black Nativity.

DECEMBER 9–11: Trolley light tours, winter celebrations at the Children's Museum, menorah lighting, Christmas concert at the Old North Church, and the Jingle Bell Run to benefit the Massachusetts Special Olympics.

DECEMBER 30–JANUARY 2: New Year's Eve Pops Concert, First Night Boston, First Day.

CHICAGO, ILLINOIS

Chicago Convention and Tourism Bureau, (312) 567-8500.
DECEMBER: Christmas Remembered Holiday Display, Chicago Botanic Garden; (718) 835-5440.
DECEMBER: Caroling to the Animals, Lincoln Park Zoo; (312) 935-6700.
DECEMBER: Holiday Lights Festival, North Michigan Avenue from Chicago River to Oak Street; (312) 642-3570.

CINCINNATI, OHIO

Greater Cincinnati and Northern Kentucky Convention and Visitors Bureaus, (800) 344-3445 or (513) 621-6994.
NOVEMBER 18–DECEMBER 30: Festival of Lights, Cincinnati Zoo; (513) 559-7721.

DECEMBER 4: Carolfest, sponsored by the Cincinnati Music Festival Association; (513) 381-3300.

DECEMBER 11: Sleigh Bells and Storytime, a holiday event for children at the William Howard Taft National Historical Site; (513) 684-3262.

DECEMBER 15: World's Largest Office Party, a charitable event at the Cincinnati Hyatt Regency, benefiting three children's charities; (513) 579-1234.

DENVER, COLORADO

The Denver Metro Convention and Visitors Bureau, (303) 892-1505.
DECEMBER–JANUARY: Blossom of Lights, Denver Botanic Garden; (303) 331-4010.

DECEMBER: Parade of Lights, a two-mile parade through downtown Denver; (303) 534-1053.

DECEMBER: Christmas with the Colorado Children's Choir; (303) 892-4100.

INDIANAPOLIS, INDIANA

Indianapolis City Center, (800) 323-INDY or (317) 237-5206.
NOVEMBER 25: Celebrations of Lights/Tree Lighting Ceremony, Monument Circle; (317) 237-2222.
NOVEMBER 25–DECEMBER 31: Toy Soldiers Playground Exhibit, Indiana State Museum; (317) 232-1637.
DECEMBER 11: Arthritis Foundation Jingle Bell Run; (317) 274-3518.

LITTLE ROCK, ARKANSAS

Little Rock Convention and Visitors Bureau, (501) 376-4781.
DECEMBER: Downtown Little Rock Christmas Parade, downtown Little Rock; (501) 375-0121.
DECEMBER: Capitol Lighting Ceremony, State Capitol; (501) 682-1001.
DECEMBER: Holiday Pops, Arkansas Symphony Orchestra; (501) 666-1761.

LOUISVILLE, KENTUCKY

Louisville/Jefferson County Convention and Visitors Bureau, in state (800) 633-3384, out of state (800) 626-5646.

NOVEMBER 22–DECEMBER 31: *It's a Wonderful Life,* Derby Dinner Playhouse; (812) 288-8291.

DECEMBER 3: Children's Holiday Parade, Main Street, Louisville; (502) 584-6383.

DECEMBER 16–23, 26–30: Winterlight Safari, Louisville Zoo; (503) 459-2181.

MEMPHIS, TENNESSEE

Memphis Visitors Information Center, (901) 543-5333.

NOVEMBER 24–DECEMBER 4: The Enchanted Forest with Its Festival of Trees; (901) 755-TREE.

MID-NOVEMBER–JANUARY: City Sidewalks, a number of different events celebrating the holiday season. For a schedule, call (901) 543-5333.

DECEMBER: Merry Christmas Memphis Parade; (901) 526-6840.

MONTREAL, CANADA

Greater Montreal Convention and Tourism Bureau, (514) 844-5400.
DECEMBER–JANUARY: Christmas Traditions and Legends Throughout the World, Montreal Botanical Garden; (514) 872-1400.
DECEMBER–JANUARY: International Christmas Tree Exhibition, Montreal Museum of Fine Arts; (514) 285-1600.
DECEMBER–JANUARY: The Wonder Kingdom, a festival for youths ages five to seventeen, Montreal Convention Center; (514) 392-1414.

NEW YORK CITY, NEW YORK

New York Convention and Visitors Bureau, (212) 484-1200.
NOVEMBER 24: Macy's Sixty-Eighth Annual Thanksgiving Day Parade; (212) 494-4414.
NOVEMBER–DECEMBER: Holiday store window displays at Saks Fifth Avenue, Macy's, Lord & Taylor.

NOVEMBER–DECEMBER: The Christmas Spectacular with the Rockettes, Radio City Music Hall; (212) 632-4085.

DECEMBER: Lighting of the Christmas tree at Rockefeller Center; (212) 632-3975.

DECEMBER: Kwanzaa Holiday Expo, an African Celebration, Jacob K. Javits Convention Center; (718) 992-9933.

DECEMBER 31: *Runner's World* Midnight Run, Central Park; (212) 860-4455.

PHILADELPHIA, PENNSYLVANIA

Philadelphia Convention and Visitors Bureau, (212) 636-3300.

DECEMBER–JANUARY: *The Nutcracker,* Pennsylvania Ballet; (215) 551-7000.

DECEMBER 31: Neighbors in the New Year, a holiday celebration with fireworks over the Delaware River.

JANUARY 1: Annual Mummer's Parade, Broad Street, Philadelphia.

OTTAWA, CANADA

Ottawa Tourism and Convention Authority, (613) 237-5150.
DECEMBER–JANUARY: Christmas Lights Across Canada, Parliament Hill/Confederation Boulevard; (613) 239-5000.
DECEMBER 31: First Night Ottawa, a celebration with members of the local arts community, at Sparks Street Mall and other locations; (613) 231-7303.

PHOENIX, ARIZONA

Phoenix and Valley of the Sun Convention and Visitors Bureau, (602) 254-6500.
DECEMBER: Luminaria Night, Desert Botanical Garden; (602) 941-1225.
DECEMBER: Old-fashioned Ornament Making, Pioneer Arizona Living History Museum; (602) 993-5071.
DECEMBER: Annual Christmas lighting/decorating contest, Payson; (602) 474-4515.

PORTLAND, OREGON

Portland Oregon Visitors Association, (503) 222-2223.

DECEMBER 2–30: Annual Festival of Lights at the Grotto, the largest choral festival in the Pacific Northwest; (503) 254-7371.

DECEMBER 3: Historic Oregon City's Annual Main Street Holiday Parade and Trail's End Lighting Event, Oregon City; (503) 650-6010.

DECEMBER 3–31: OMSI's Annual Winter Solstice Renaissance Festival, Oregon Museum of Science and Industry; (503) 797-4000.

DECEMBER 16: Annual Figgy Pudding Corner Caroling Competition; (503) 223-2223.

RALEIGH/DURHAM, NORTH CAROLINA

North Carolina Travel and Tourism Division, in state (919) 733-4171, out of state (800) VISIT-NC.

DECEMBER 11–12: Christmas in Scandinavia, Durham Civil Choral Society; (919) 968-4914.

DECEMBER 11–15: Christmas by Candlelight, Duke Homestead, Durham; (919) 477-5498.

DECEMBER 31: First Night Raleigh, downtown Raleigh, family entertainment; (919) 831-6221.

SAN FRANCISCO, CALIFORNIA

San Francisco Convention and Visitors Bureau, (415) 974-6900.

NOVEMBER: Tree lightings, Ghiradelli Square; (415) 435-8811.

NOVEMBER: Tree lighting, Union Square; (415) 781-7880.

DECEMBER: Santa Claus Parade, Mission District; (415) 826-1401.

DECEMBER: Celebration of Christmas Past, Western Addison Society, shows how a Victorian Christmas was once celebrated in San Francisco; (415) 974-9320.

SEATTLE, WASHINGTON

Seattle-King County Convention and Visitors Bureau, (206) 461-5800.

DECEMBER: Christmas Traditions in Scandinavia, Ballard; (206) 789-5707.

DECEMBER: Christmas Celebration, Seattle; (206) 623-0340.
DECEMBER: Times Square of the West New Year's Eve Celebration; (206) 443-9700.

TORONTO, CANADA.

Metropolitan Toronto Convention and Visitors Association, (800) 363-1990 or (416) 203-2500.
NOVEMBER 20: Santa Claus Parade, the world's longest-running children's parade.
DECEMBER 10–JANUARY 7: Historic Toronto Christmas, re-creates Christmas Days gone by in three historic homes.
DECEMBER 31: New Year's Eve at City Hall, Nathan Philips Square.

VANCOUVER, CANADA

Greater Vancouver Convention and Visitors Bureau, (604) 682-2222.
DECEMBER: Christmas Carolship Parade, Vancouver Harbor; (604) 682-2007.

DECEMBER 2–JANUARY 1: Festival of Lights, Van Dusen Gardens; (604) 266-7194.

DECEMBER 10–11: Country Christmas, Maplewood Farm, North Vancouver; (604) 929-5610.

WASHINGTON, D.C.

Washington, D.C. Convention and Visitors Association, (202) 789-7000.

DECEMBER 3–5: An American Holiday Celebration, the U.S. Army Band, D.A.R. Constitution Hall; (703) 696-3399.

DECEMBER 8–JANUARY 1: Pageant of Peace, a series of events at locations around the city. It includes the National Christmas Tree Lighting (December 8), nightly choral performances, yule logs, a nativity, and Christmas trees representing each state and territory in the United States; (202) 619-7222.

DECEMBER 18–JANUARY 1: Christmas Poinsettia Show, U.S. Botanic Garden; (202) 226-4082.

DECEMBER (throughout): Christmas celebration and services, Washington National Cathedral; (202) 537-6200.

Making
Spirits Bright:
Charitable
Giving

As a youngster, you probably viewed the approach of the Christmas season with great anticipation, wondering what presents would be under the tree. Maybe, if you were good, everything you wanted would be there on Christmas morning. Certainly most of us can remember the excitement of Christmas Day, hoping that Santa did believe we were good all year, and that the reward for this stellar behavior would be downstairs in the form of a bicycle or a sled.

But as you grow older, you may find yourself questioning the time, expense, and purpose of all the frenetic spending that goes on during Christmas. Although you may not want to skimp on the presents for your children or nieces and nephews, you may prefer to take a different approach to the gifts you give to the adults on your Christmas list.

There are many forms of charitable giving that can be combined with or substituted for gift giving. You can buy presents from organizations raising money for worthy causes or give cash to a friend's favorite charity in lieu of buying him or her a gift. Or you and your friends can get together to buy presents for a family who can't afford to celebrate Christmas, instead of exchanging gifts among yourselves.

A good many worthwhile causes need the financial support of the public. But it's all too easy to overlook a solicitation for money—especially from a little-known group—during the Christmas season, when you're trying to stay within a budget. Don't do this. Giving to a charity or nonprofit organization in the name of a friend or family member can help spread the message of the season beyond your own close circle.

If you choose to give money to a charity instead of buying gifts, keep a couple of things in mind. First, you'll want to choose an organization that reflects the concerns or interests of the person or family in whose name you're donating the money. Second, you should learn how your donations will be used. Ask a few questions before you send in the check: What percentage of the money goes to the organization's goals? What percentage goes to administration? Organizations that funnel more money into their administrative activities, rather than delivering the education, medical care, or food they purport to, may not be as effective in carrying out their goals. Also ask what kind of functions your money will support. Do you endorse these sorts of activities? Do your friends agree with the purpose of this group? Double-check how the funds are used, and ask for a financial statement or an annual report.

When making a donation, don't send cash or use your credit card. And finally, don't forget to keep clear records of your donations since they are often tax deductible.

What follows is a list of charities taken from the Council of Better Business Bureau's *Annual Charity Index*. The charities on the list meet all of the twenty-two standards set out by the CBBB. These standards include: public accountability, use of funds, solicitations and informational materials, fund-raising practices and governance. To receive your own copy of the *Annual Charity Index*, send a check or money order for $12.95, made payable to the Council of Better Business Bureaus, to:

> Charity Index, Council of Better Business Bureaus, 4200 Wilson Boulevard, Suite 800, Arlington, VA 22203; or call (703) 276-0100.

The CBBB's *Index* is made up of the charities that the CBBB's Philanthropic Advisory Service most frequently receives inquiries about. It does not, however, indicate which charities meet all of the CBBB's standards. To get an up-to-date list of those organizations that do meet the CBBB's criteria, order a copy of the CBBB's *Give But Give Wisely*, a bimonthly publication that provides information and guidance about charitable giving.

The following charities are by no means the only organizations where your money will be used wisely. Don't forget your local library, schools, hospitals, police and firefighters' groups, or local parks at Christmastime. There are a number of wonderful and deserving organizations that may not have been included in the CBBB's publications because they are local rather than national. Ask your state or local division of the CBBB if it has information on local charities you're interested in supporting. Also check the charity indexes at your local library.

The list that follows is broken down into seven categories: animal and wildlife groups; children's groups; environmental groups; health organizations involved in both research and education; human services groups, which provide counseling, crisis care, as well as assistance for the disabled; international relief organizations; veterans' groups; and other organizations, including those involved in education, civil rights, food, housing, and drug abuse.

Animal and Wildlife Groups

Animal Legal Defense Fund, 1363 Lincoln Avenue, Suite 7, San Rafael, CA 94901; (415) 459-0885.
Works for the protection and promotion of animal rights.

Defenders of Wildlife, 1224 Nineteenth Street, NW, Washington, DC 20036; (202) 659-9510.
Works to educate the public about wildlife issues, as well as to protect endangered species and their habitats.

Humane Society of the United States, 2100 L Street, NW, Washington, DC 20037; (202) 452-1100.

Improves the quality of life for all livestock, wildlife, laboratory animals, and pets on local, regional, and national levels.

Wildlife Habitat Canada, 1704 Carling Avenue, Suite 301, Ottawa, Ontario, Canada K2A 1C7; (613) 722-2090. *Works with private landowners, governmental, and nongovernmental organizations to protect Canada's wildlife by conserving animal habitats.*

Children's Groups

Boys and Girls Clubs of America, 771 First Avenue, New York, NY 10017; (212) 351-5900. *Provides advisory services to community groups that sponsor programs for young people in recreation, job training, and the prevention of alcohol and drug abuse.*

Boys Town/Father Flanagan's Boys' Home, 14100 Crawford Street, Boys Town, NE 68010; (402) 498-1300.

Gives food, clothing, shelter, education, spiritual guidance, and medical care to abused, handicapped, and homeless youth.

Children Incorporated, 1000 Westover Road, Richmond, VA 23220; (804) 359-4562.
Provides food, clothing, shelter, education, and medical assistance to needy children in the United States and overseas.

Make a Wish Foundation, 100 West Clarendon, Suite 2200, Phoenix, AZ 85013; (800) 722-9474.
Grants wishes to children under the age of eighteen who have life-threatening illnesses.

Environmental Groups

Canadian Parks and Wilderness Society, Wildlands League, 160 Bloor Street East, Suite 1335, Toronto, Ontario, Canada M4W 1B9; (416) 324-9760.

Protects Canada's parks and wilderness areas.

Center for Marine Conservation, 1725 DeSales Street, NW, Suite 500, Washington, DC 20036; (202) 429-5609.
Works to conserve marine habitats, prevent marine pollution, and protect endangered marine life.

National Arbor Day Foundation, 211 N. Twelfth Street, Suite 501, Lincoln, NE 68508; (402) 474-5655.
Encourages tree planting and educates people about the conservation of trees throughout America.

Nature Conservancy, 1815 North Lynn Street, Arlington, VA 22209; (703) 841-5300.
Works to preserve rare and endangered species by protecting natural land and waters.

Wilderness Society, 900 Seventeenth Street, NW, Washington, DC 20006; (202) 833-2300.

Strives to preserve wilderness and wildlife in America and to gain support for environmental issues.

Health Organizations

American Institute for Cancer Research, 1759 R Street, NW, Washington, DC 20009; (202) 328-7744.
Works to educate the public about cancer. Also funds research on the causes and treatments of the disease, specifically the link between cancer and diet.

American Kidney Fund, 6110 Executive Boulevard, Suite 1010, Rockville, MD 20852; (800) 638-8299.
Provides direct financial assistance, educational programs, research grants, and community services for people with kidney disease.

Leukemia Society of America, 600 Third Avenue, New York, NY 10016; (212) 573-8484.

Promotes and supports research into causes, cures, and treatments for leukemia and related diseases.

National Multiple Sclerosis Society, 733 Third Avenue, New York, NY 10017; (212) 986-3240.
Works to prevent, treat, and cure MS and to improve the quality of life for both individuals with MS and their families.

Human Services Groups

The Association for Retarded Citizens of the U.S./The ARC, 500 East Border Street, Suite 300, Arlington, TX 76010; (817) 261-6003.
Strives to improve the welfare of the mentally retarded and their families, as well as to reduce the incidence of mental retardation.

Covenant House, 346 West Seventeenth Street, New York, NY 10011; (212) 727-4000.

Provides crisis care to homeless and runaway youths under twenty-one years of age.

Guiding Eyes for the Blind, 611 Granite Springs Road, Yorktown Heights, NY 10598; (904) 254-4024.
Works to provide greater mobility for visually handicapped people through professionally trained guidedogs.

Mays Mission for the Handicapped, 604 Colonial Drive, Heber Springs, AR 72543; (501) 362-7526.
Provides employment and other services for handicapped persons, along with spiritual guidance.

International Relief Organizations

Americares Foundation, 161 Cherry Street, New Canaan, CT 06840; (203) 966-5195.

Gives emergency relief and medical aid to communities around the world in need of disaster relief.

International Church Relief Fund, 182 Farmers Lane, Santa Rosa, CA 95405; (707) 528-8000.
Provides nutritional, medical, and material support and disaster relief to underdeveloped countries.

Map International, 2200 Glynco Parkway, P.O. Box 50, Brunswick, GA 31521; (912) 265-6010.
Supplies emergency relief to other countries. Also helps develop assistance projects to missions in developing countries and provides health-related workers with short-term overseas service projects.

World Relief Corporation, P.O. Box WRC, Wheaton, IL 60189; (708) 665-0235.
Helps people in developing countries through relief and

development projects. Also provides food, clothing, and medicine.

Veterans' Groups

Amvets National Service Foundation, 4647 Forbes Boulevard, Lanham, MD 20706; (301) 459-6181.
Provides financial aid for AMVETS' programs, the goals of which are to help American veterans and their families.

Blinded Veterans Association, 477 H Street NW, Washington DC 20001; (202) 371-8880.
Promotes the welfare of blinded and visually impaired veterans of the U.S. Armed Forces.

Other Organizations

Amnesty International. In the United States: 322 Eighth Avenue, New York, NY 10001; (800) AMNESTY. In

Canada: 130 Slater Street, Suite 900, Ottawa, Ontario K1P 6E2; (613) 563-1891.

Works to release people who've been imprisoned wrongly, because of race, religion, sex, age, or beliefs. Also attempts to improve prison conditions and to abolish torture and execution.

Association of American Indian Affairs, 245 Fifth Avenue, New York, NY 10016; (212) 689-8720.

Promotes the welfare of Native Americans and Alaska Natives by protecting their rights, natural resources, and by improving their health, education, and economic development.

Christian Appalachian Project, 322 Crab Orchard Road, Lancaster, KY 40446; (606) 792-3051.

Provides social and economic programs to the underprivileged in Appalachia through education, job training, and emergency aid.

National Trust for Historic Preservation, 1785 Massachusetts Avenue NW, Washington, DC 20036; (202) 673-
4000.

*Works to promote the American heritage and to help preserve
historic buildings, objects, and communities.*

In addition to the above suggestions, there are many organizations out there that could use your donation at Christmas and
throughout the year. Numerous organizations fund research for
or work with people who have AIDS, cancer, muscular dystrophy,
and cerebral palsy. And don't forget to look into making donations
to local charities or smaller nonprofit institutions.

Another source for charitable giving is the *Alternative Gift Catalog,* published by Alternative Gift Markets, an interfaith, nonprofit
Christian ministry. The catalog profiles a number of charitable
organizations to which you can make specific donations, that will
fund such worthy projects as preserving one acre of rain forest,
providing literacy and hygiene training for a person in Nepal,

giving job counseling to a homeless person in the United States, or providing tuition for schoolchildren in Haiti. For a copy of the catalog, write to:

Alternative Gift Markets, Inc.
20646 Highway 18
Apple Valley, CA 92307

or call (800) 842-2243.

GIFTS THAT
KEEP ON GIVING:
SUPPORTING
GOOD WORKS

When you're thinking of where you need to start your Christmas shopping, your first thought might be "at the mall." But keep in mind you can make your money go farther by buying gifts from organizations that sell goods to raise money for the causes they work to support, like protecting the environment or working for human rights. Many groups sell reasonably priced goods, with

74

part of each sale's proceeds going to support the group's activities or other nonprofit organizations whose work the group endorses.

Because thrift is part of the theme of *Simply Christmas,* the gifts suggested here are typically under $20, though there are a few that come in a little higher. Also included are retailers that sell environmentally friendly goods, because buying these goods helps keep the world a little cleaner.

What follows is a list of mail-order retailers that donate a portion of their profits to their own work or that of other nonprofit organizations. Some of these retailers may have outlets near you, but in the event they don't, refer to the phone numbers provided to request a copy of their catalog. Remember, if you're shopping by mail, start early.

All Things Wise and Wonderful, Inc., P.O. Box 267, Pierrefonds Station, Pierrefonds, Quebec, Canada H9H 4K9; (514) 683-8407.

You have to send C$2 to receive this catalog, but that money is refunded with your first order. All Things Wise and Wonderful sells environmentally friendly products ranging from nightshirts to crystal stone deodorants. It also stocks gourmet foods, cosmetics, and natural insect repellents. It's a "green" general store with plenty of reasonably priced products that would be welcomed by many of your friends.

The Art Institute of Chicago, The Museum Shop, 111 South Michigan Avenue, Chicago, IL 60603-6110; (800) 621-9337.

In addition to the Museum of Modern Art in New York and Boston's Museum of Fine Arts, mentioned earlier, the Art Institute is a great source for Christmas cards and gifts. It sells cards, jewelry, books, and prints for under $20. It also sells a beautiful Advent calendar ($11.95)—a perfect gift for the season. (Don't forget to stop by the museums in smaller towns as well as big cities. And remember that museum memberships make great gifts; consider giving one to an art-loving family or friend.)

Better Homes Foundation; (800) 962-4676.

At Christmastime, the Better Homes Foundation sells a couple of products, the proceeds of which fund its work to place homeless families in permanent housing. For example, it sells beeswax candles that are made by homeless people. These candles cost about $9 for a box of two eight-inch candles, and almost $4 of the purchase price goes to support the foundation's work. The gifts may change from year to year, so call the toll-free number to see what is on the foundation's list for Christmas 1994, or pick up an issue of *Better Homes and Gardens,* where you can find pictures and prices for the goods.

The Body Shop Catalog, The Body Shop by Mail, 452 Horsehill Road, Cedar Knolls, NJ 07927-2014; (800) 541-2535.

The Body Shop sells soaps, creams, brushes, bath products, makeup, and other personal-care products. Prices vary depending on the product, but there are many goods priced under $20 that would make great Christmas gifts. Consider a kit that includes the Body Shop's Peppermint Foot Lotion and a Footsie Roller ($13.95), or a sampling of the company's three best-selling products (Fuzzy Peach Shower Gel, Peppermint Foot Lotion, Fuzzy Peach Soap) for $14.95. For the kids on your list, consider a gift box of Endangered Species soaps. Each kit contains five animal soaps in the shape of an endangered species; it also includes an educational leaflet telling the child what he or she can do to help save this animal—all for only $8.25.

Some of the profits go toward helping communities around the world, either by supporting new business initiatives or by providing educational programs for the company's employees and its customers. The Body Shop also supports nonprofit organizations like Amnesty International, which works to free people who have been wrongly imprisoned. In addition, Body Shop customers are encouraged to bring in their used bottles for refills, to cut down on waste. Finally, the company's products are minimally packaged, which also helps to reduce waste.

When you finish with the catalog, the company asks that you pass it on to a friend or bring it to one of its stores to be recycled.

Bridgehead, 20 James Street, Ottawa, Ontario, Canada K2P 0T6; (800) 565-8563; fax (613) 567-1468.

Bridgehead is an arm of Oxfam-Canada, a nonprofit organization devoted to educating the public about world hunger and to setting up self-development and disaster relief programs in Africa, Asia, Latin America, and the Caribbean. Bridgehead is Oxfam Canada's retail outlet and sells goods made in third-world countries. Its catalog features gift items like jewelry, clothing, and toys, as well as greeting cards.

The Company of Women, 102 Main Street, Nyack, NY 10960-0742; (800) 937-1193.

Proceeds from the sale of products ordered through this catalog generate funds for the programs of the Rockland, New York, Family Shelter. This is an agency serving victims of domestic violence, rape survivors, and the homeless.

Gifts range from clocks to pillows, from T-shirts (printed with inspirational messages) to security devices. For $15 or less, you could order a Meditations Journal ($13.00); a Girls Can Do Anything Poster, suitable for the young girl on your list, which comes with a set of fifteen water-base markers for coloring ($15.00); or a group of five magnetic car safety signs ($9.95), which signal to passing motorists what kind of trouble you're in if you've pulled over (e.g., "flat," "medical," or "gas").

Co-op America, 1850 M Street NW, Suite 700, P.O. Box 18217, Washington DC 20036; (202) 223-1881.

Co-op America's catalog features a number of goods made by a variety of projects around the world. These projects work with small businesses to foster rural economic development. They also help Native Americans establish economic independence by creating and developing small businesses. The profits from the sales also go to groups that teach job skills to homeless people and to those that set up alternative trade organizations in developing countries, the products of which you can buy through the catalog. In addition, Co-op America's catalog features a number of environmentally friendly products.

Because many of the goods are handmade and imported, Co-op America asks that you do your Christmas ordering by November 30 so your items will arrive in time for the holidays.

The products the catalog sells range from clothes to food to "green" underwear, all for under $20. Remember that depending on what you buy, proceeds from your purchase will go to support the business that produced it. For example, from the Women's Bean Project in Denver, which provides jobs and job training for homeless women in Denver, you could buy soup mixes and pasta salad ingredients. Each of these products comes dried, in its own wooden box complete with recipes, and costs only $15.

You could send a family on your list a box of fruits and nuts from the Brazilian rain forests, all harvested by people who've depended on the rain forest for their livelihood for generations. A gift tin contains four seven-ounce bags and costs $17.95.

Silk for Life, an organization that helps Colombian farmers switch from raising cocaine to raising silk, sells the silk and wool gloves and socks. Prices range from $13 to $15.

You could give someone on your list a set of four hand-block batiked napkins ($13.95) from Marketplace of India. Marketplace of India is a fair-trade group that works with physically challenged people and low-income artisans from the slums of Bombay.

The catalog also features T-shirts, books, and other goods, all of which are made by people trying to better their lives or by groups supporting budding economies and those working to preserve the environment.

Earth General, 72 Seventh Avenue, Brooklyn, NY 11217-3649; (800) 562-2203, in New York City (718) 398-4648.

Through its store and catalog, Earth General sells a variety of environmentally friendly products ranging from untreated, organic bedding to recycled glassware. For under $20, you can buy those on your list natural cotton dishtowels, potholders, aprons, or reusable lunchbags. For children, there are a number of games, as well as papermaking kits, wooden toys, coloring books, and natural crayon sets. Earth General also sells candles made by Light Up America, a New York–based organization that employs homeless people to make the candles. Proceeds from the sale of these candles go toward refurbishing abandoned houses to house the homeless. Prices for the candles range from $5.99 to $11.99.

EPI Marketing, 250 Pequot Avenue, Southport, CT 06490; (800) WHALE93 or (203) 255-1112.

When you buy a gift made by EPI Marketing, 5 to 20 percent of the proceeds from the sale will be donated to conservation groups so that they can continue their work. The groups EPI supports are the Nature Conservancy, the World Wildlife Fund, the Earth Island Institute, and the United States Fish and Wildlife Service. EPI Marketing sells Earthmates, reversible stuffed animals that can be turned into globes. The stuffed animals cost $19.95, and by buying one stuffed animal you will help preserve twenty-five square feet of endangered rain-forest habitat or generate funds for the Earth Island Institute or the International Wildlife Coalition. How your money is used depends on whether you buy a Jurassic Dino Globe, a dolphin, whale, polar bear, or monkey.

EPI Marketing also sells, among other things, coffee mugs ($7.95) and whale adoption kits ($19.95).

Forestsaver, Inc., P.O. Box 610264, Bayside, NY 11361; (800) 777-9886.

Forestsaver sells MAPelopes, which are colorful stationery and envelopes made from surplus maps. A set includes fifty-five sheets of stationery, eighteen envelopes, and twenty-eight address labels, all for $10.95. In addition, the company sells journals, coloring books, gift wrap, and eco-writer pencils which are made from 100 percent recycled cardboard and paper. Save a tree, and get these goods for the letter writers on your list.

The Metropolitan Museum of Art, 255 Gracie Station, New York, NY 10028-9998; (800) 468-7376.

Another great source for sophisticated but inexpensive gifts. Posters for budding artists, Christmas cards, silver candle snuffers, dishes, address books, and games are all available through this catalog for less than $20.

National Wildlife Federation, 1400 Sixteenth Street, NW, Washington DC 20077-9964; (800) 432-6564.

The NWF sells T-shirts, mugs, jewelry, and games for the children and teenagers on your list. You could also give a child a subscription to the two magazines published by the NWF. *Your Big Back Yard* is an activity magazine for children ages three to five and costs $12 for a year's subscription. A year's subscription to *Ranger Rick* costs $15 and qualifies the recipient for a junior membership in the NWF.

The Paper Source, General Delivery, Fallbrook, Ontario, Canada K0G 1A0; (800) 665-1143 or (613) 267-7191.

If you give stationery to a friend or family member, make sure it's made of recycled paper. You don't need to look any farther than this catalog to find notepaper, cards, office paper, and envelopes for the people on your list. The Paper Source also sells Christmas cards.

Royal Ontario Museum, 100 Queen's Park, Toronto, Ontario, Canada M4S2C6; (416) 586-5842.

Each September the museum publishes a catalog for the Christmas season. It sells prints, posters, jewelry, as well as glassware, games, and toys.

Signals, WGBH Educational Foundation, P.O. Box 64428, St. Paul, MN 55164-0428; (800) 669-9696.

This catalog is a publication of WGBH Educational Foundation in Boston, which supports public television. It has a wonderful selection of videos to choose from, including classic PBS productions of *The Scarlet Pimpernel* and *The Merchant of Venice*. It also sells videos by British star John Cleese, such as the *How to Irritate People Video* and *John Cleese: The Strange Case of the End of Civilization Video*. These videos sell for about $20.

Along with a great video selection, the catalog offers a wide range of gifts within your price range. Why not have your child make a special tie for Dad with Signals Design a Tie ($19.95)? The tie comes with five magic markers and a practice swatch. Maybe someone on your list has been wanting to learn a foreign language. If so, consider buying a set of language tapes that provides basic instruction in speaking conversationally in one of nineteen foreign languages ($18.95). Each set comes with two audiocassettes, each of which is an hour and a half long, and a phrase dictionary. The catalog also sells a number of books to help improve skills in spelling, public speaking, and grammar.

Additional craft items that would make great gifts include an iron Sun Candleholder ($12.95) and a Make a Plate and Make a Mug Set ($19.95), which lets you or your children personalize a plate and mug for grandparents, aunts, or uncles.

Starbucks Coffee, 2203 Airport Way South, P.O. Box 34510, Seattle, WA 98124-1510; (800) 782-7282.

Starbucks offers a wide variety of coffees, as well as coffee-making and -drinking paraphernalia you can send to the java lovers on your list. It's included in this section because it sells the perfect gift for those who are interested in spreading the wealth around. Starbucks Care Sampler ($18.95) features four half-pound bags of coffee from the different countries Starbucks and CARE have been working with. Starbucks donates $2 to CARE for each Starbucks CARE Sampler sold. So keep this company in mind for the adults on your list.

Very Special Arts, Very Special Arts Holiday Collection, P.O. Box 428, Taylor, MI 48180; (800) 866-8VSA.

Very Special Arts is an international organization providing programs in the arts for disabled individuals. VSA has programs in fifty-five countries and works to promote awareness of the educational and cultural benefits of the arts for all people. Its holiday catalog features Christmas ornaments made by participants of the VSA programs in India (four for $4), holiday notecards featuring the artwork of VSA artists (fifteen for $10), and T-shirts printed with the work of artists who work with VSA ($10 to $15 depending on the size).

Remember that some of the other organizations that were mentioned earlier, like UNICEF and Amnesty International, sell gifts through their catalogs as well. But also bear in mind that you do not necessarily have to contact a group working to save the environment or helping needy children in order to find gifts that "keep on giving." Such gifts can come directly from you. These days, our lives are so busy with work, family, and just getting little things in order, that time has become a precious commodity. Consequently, a gift of your time would be a special gift to many people in your life.

For example, spend an afternoon with one of the children on

your list. Plan a trip to a destination that the child selects. Perhaps a movie or play would be just the ticket. One great afternoon can mean a whole lot more than a toy or new clothes.

You could also offer to baby-sit for a couple who doesn't get out much. Give them a booklet of baby-sitting certificates good for several nights during the year. Chances are this would be one of the most treasured gifts they'd receive during the holidays.

If one of your elderly relatives is in a nursing home or can't get out of the house very often, why not serve as a chauffeur for a day? Take your relative to a mall so he or she can do some shopping without worrying about transportation.

People who have certain skills, such as being handy around the house, could offer their services to a friend who needs something repaired. Artists could offer to spend an hour with a child or adult who's interested in learning how to draw or paint.

Even if you don't have specific skills, you could volunteer to help a family with a big project like painting a room or helping with yardwork during the spring. You could also cook a big dinner for someone. The recipient might freeze it for another night or eat it on the spot—and you would clean up afterward. Some moms and dads would probably love a night away from the kitchen.

If you have a car and a friend doesn't, offer to drive somewhere your friend needs to go. Like the baby-sitting certificates, a book of coupons entitling your friend to use your driving services at a future date would make a wonderful gift.

Friends who live in the city might appreciate a weekend at your home in the suburbs or the country. A friend who's throwing a party could certainly use some help: Offer to serve, bartend, run errands, or clean up afterward.

Keep in mind those people around you who may not have friends or family to spend Christmas with. If you know someone who will be alone during the holidays, why not invite this person to share Christmas dinner with you?

Remember, giving your time can be one of the easiest things you can do, and can also be one of the most appreciated.

Santa on a
Shoestring Budget:
Gifts for Under
$20

A year's worth of wishes fulfilled in one day—that's probably what Christmas held for you when you were a child. All that you asked for might be found under the family tree on Christmas morning, provided you'd been good all year long.

A Christmas celebration would feel incomplete without presents. Though in a busy life a holiday without them might seem like a blessing: It would free you from the hassle of shopping, wrapping, and shipping. Nevertheless, gift giving is a lovely expression of love and friendship that's central to the holiday.

With this in mind, *Simply Christmas* offers a list of gift suggestions to make Christmas shopping easier, by freeing up your time and providing you with a game plan before you begin this annual ritual.

When you do your Christmas shopping, use your imagination. Expense is no substitute for creativity or thoughtfulness. Keep in mind what people need but might not have bought themselves. What are their hobbies or interests? Is there something you could buy them that would encourage them to begin a hobby?

Before you go out to buy the gifts, make a list of all the people you need to buy presents for. Then list two or three gifts you feel would be appropriate for each person. Getting an idea of what you're looking for beforehand will save you time and probably money, because you won't end up reaching for an expensive item as a last-minute substitute because you're unsure of what to buy. Once you've gotten your list together, call ahead to stores to see if they have the item, and don't forget to ask the price.

If you are stumped by what to get certain people on your list, consider buying them "standby" gifts like books or videos, or making them a batch of cookies delivered in a new tin or cookie jar that can be used again. Framed photographs are always welcome, as are Christmas ornaments or other decorative items that can be used during the holiday.

It's important to set a budget before you begin your shopping. Keeping within your budget will make the following winter months more bearable since you won't be saddled with a huge credit-card bill from the holiday season.

To save yourself time during Christmas, and to avoid the Christmas rush, try to buy gifts throughout the year. And keep an eye out for decorative containers, pretty jars, or tins you can use to package gifts of food. Even if you don't have anyone in particular in mind when you buy an item that catches your eye, chances are when the holidays roll around, it will make a great fallback present. Also, try to collect things over the year. Is there a child on your list who collects coins, buttons, or matchbooks? How about seashells, playing cards, or rocks? Put these in a small display case and add a book on whatever it is the child is interested in, and you have a great, inexpensive Christmas gift.

What are the best places to buy gifts—*aside from* the malls? Check out the crafts fairs that are held during the Christmas season in many towns, and which feature goods made by local artisans. These can be a great source of inexpensive and unusual gifts. Look through your newspaper for notices about auctions and estate sales as well. Here you may be able to pick up prints, glassware, plates, or jewelry for the people on your list. Also remember that you could get some of your Christmas shopping done at the many church and school bazaars held at Christmastime.

Books are great gifts. But don't limit yourself to shopping in the big bookstore chains. Secondhand bookstores are less expensive and often have titles that are out of print and can't be found in the big chains. Additionally, these stores may sell old prints or maps that you could have framed for your family members or friends.

Hardware stores, housewares stores, and Asian import stores

carry a wide variety of inexpensive houseware items. Consider such gifts as a set of plastic glasses for the patio, a bunch of different kitchen items like garlic presses, cheese knives, or wooden spoons you tie together with a red bow. This way, your friends will have all the utensils they need the next time they throw a dinner party.

Because catalogs are a convenient and increasingly popular source of gifts, one section of this chapter is devoted to mail-order retailers that sell practical and unusual gifts for $20 or less. Other sections are organized by the age group of the recipient, providing inexpensive gift suggestions for the children, teenagers, and adults on your Christmas list.

Mail-Order Gifts

Catalogs are a great source of gift ideas. And during the holiday rush, many of these companies can save you time by wrapping and shipping the present for you. So shopping can be as simple as choosing the item and making a phone call. Of course, the wrapping costs a little extra, but the price may be worth the time you save.

If you'll be using direct mail, start early—as early as late October or early November. Many of these retailers require the gift be ordered three weeks before Christmas to ensure it arrives on time, but if you wait that long, your item may be out of stock. So try to place your orders before Thanksgiving. If you're stuck, many of the direct-mail retailers will ship their goods via an express-mail service, but this can be expensive.

The following list is a short one. There are literally hundreds of direct-mail retailers in the United States and Canada. If you're interested in finding out about other catalogs, check your local library for indexes or associations of mail-order retailers. Or get a copy of the *Catalog Handbook* or *The Original Catalogue of Canadian Catalogues*. These publications are discussed below, followed by an alphabetical listing of specific catalogs.

The Catalog Handbook, Enterprise Magazines of Milwaukee; (414) 272-9977.

You can pick up this catalog at most magazine stands for $4. *The Catalog Handbook* doesn't sell anything; it just lists a lot of different catalogs that sell the items you may be looking for. Best of all, many of the entries are offbeat catalogs, like the one from Status for Sale—(800) 257-8288—which sells nobility titles and backstage passes to concerts. A more conventional entry is that for Apple-source—(217) 245-7589—which sells eighty varieties of apples.

The Original Catalogue of Canadian Catalogues, by Leila Albala, Alpel Publishing, P.O. Box 203, Chambly, Quebec, Canada J3L 4B3; (514) 658-6205; fax (514) 658-3514.

With listings of more than 800 mail-order sources, this little book is a must for Canadian readers looking to avoid the crowds during the Christmas shopping season. The catalog provides its readers with sources for gifts ranging from religious articles to fly-fishing gear to products for left-handed people. Making the small investment in this book (C$9.95) can save you a lot of time and money. To order the next edition, give your name and address to the company; you'll be put on a mailing list and contacted when it's available.

American Spoon Foods, 1668 Clarion Avenue, P.O. Box 566, Petoskey, MI 49770-0566; (800) 222-5886.

The gift packs from American Spoon Foods take the hassle out of trying to find just the right present for adults on your list. This catalog offers mouthwatering assortments of jams, spoon fruits, salad dressings, and barbecue sauces. A gift of three jars of spoon fruits or jams costs about $17.95; a trio of no-oil salad dressings, $15.95. The catalog itself is also a good source for holiday recipes. Pick a recipe you like, and send one of your friends a copy along with the mustard, dressing, or butter made by American Spoon Foods that's used in the recipe.

American Spoon Foods also sells dried fruits, marinades, pancake mixes, granola, and pasta sauces. Make a basket of your favorites to send to friends.

The Bird's Nest Mail Order, 331 Cornwallis Street, Kentville, Nova Scotia, Canada B4N 2G6; (902) 678-9514.

A good source of gifts for babies and toddlers. The catalog carries clothing, along with a number of items to decorate a child's room. It also features toys, books, and tapes for young children.

CD Plus Compact Disc Catalogue, 1825 Dundas Street East, Unit 13, Mississauga, Ontario, Canada L4X 2X1; (416) 629-9255; fax (416) 629-0414.

You can pick up this catalog at newsstands in Canada, or send C$4.95 to the above address to receive it. CD Plus carries over 27,000 music titles and will ship CDs anywhere in Canada.

Childcraft, P.O. Box 29149, Mission, KS 66201-9149; (800) 631-5667.

Those who need to buy gifts for children may be stumped during the holidays, either by the prices of games and toys, or by the overwhelming selection found in toy stores. Buying a child's gift through a catalog can make things a little easier on you, and many mail-order retailers like Childcraft will send the present to the recipient, wrapped and ready to go under the tree. The charge for this service typically runs between $2.50 to $5.00 per item.

In addition to toys and videos, Childcraft sells colorful personalized backpacks, overnight bags, and lunch bags ($12.95 to $16.95). Educational toys like Writestart, which uses thirty activities to help a child learn to write ($16.95), and a kit that puts together a twelve-page hardcover book of a child's writings or drawings ($19.95) are wonderful presents. Reasonably priced costumes, art supplies, and toys are also sold through the catalog.

Flax art & design, P.O. Box 7216, San Francisco, CA 94120-7216; (800) 547-7778.

There are a number of unusual items in this catalog that would make interesting Christmas gifts. How about an office alternative to the Swiss army knife? Flax sells an Ultra Portable Desk Tool, which is an eleven-in-one stationery organizer that contains, among other things, a ballpoint pen, hole punch, and tape measure. These and eight other gadgets are all found in this nifty 4½-by-1½-inch design ($19.00).

Those with a knack for painting might enjoy a set of nesting dolls that they can paint themselves ($12) or an all-purpose leather case for their sketching pencils ($11). Children on your list could receive ten different colored blocks of Fimo modeling clay ($9) or, if you wanted to splurge, a giant rubber stamp set with fifty-two stamps, pads, colored pencils, and crayons ($26).

If you'd like to make your own gifts, why not order a Fun Frame? The kit comes with a frame and items to decorate it with, like buttons, beads, or gems ($14 each kit, or three or more kits for $12 each).

Gardeners Eden, Mail-Order Department, P.O. Box 7307, San Francisco, CA 94120-7307; (800) 822-9600.

This is a great source of gifts for the gardeners and plant lovers on your list. Those who live in apartments may appreciate a set of four brightly colored terra-cotta pots to put on their windowsill ($13.50, plants not included). Families who have big yards and like poppies might appreciate Gardeners Eden's poppy bouquet, a seed mixture of poppies and Bishops Lace that can cover up to 200 square feet ($13.50). The catalog also offers a Fragrant Flower seed mixture for the same price.

Vases and dried flowers packed in earthenware crocks make lovely gifts ($12–$15). And for gardeners, consider the selection of tools and other gardening-related items like clogs and rose cutters for under $20.

HearthSong, 156 North Main Street, Sebastopol, CA 95472; (800) 325-2502.

For the children on your list, this is an excellent source of inexpensive but unusual gifts. While you can buy traditional toys like blocks and modeling beeswax, Hearthsong also sells books and craft kits, many of them for under $20. Some examples of what the catalog has to offer: a rubber band-powered wooden dragster, made for children over the age of three ($9.95); twelve metal puzzles, which are a great way to keep children busy on long trips ($14.95); a foxtail, which is a rubber ball with a brightly colored tail attached for throwing and catching ($10.95); an old-fashioned hobby horse ($16.95); and an Explorabook, a child's science museum within a book. The last item comes with instructions and tools for more than fifty science projects ($17.95).

Hold Everything, Mail-Order Department, P.O. Box 7807, San Francisco, CA 94120-7807; (800) 421-2264.

A good place to find gifts for the young adult who might need some things for his or her new apartment. The gadgets sold may not be at the top of anyone's Christmas list, but they are especially useful. Items include everything from floral storage boxes ($7.00 to $7.50) to plastic bags for storing sweaters or bedding ($8.00 to $16.00). Hold Everything also sells tie and belt hangers ($6.50), medicine cabinet organizers ($16.00), baskets ($16.00 to $19.00), and recipe boxes ($12.00).

The King Arthur Flour Baker's Catalogue, P.O. Box 876, Norwich, VT 05055-0876; (800) 827-6836.

For the adults or families on your Christmas list who love to cook, consider a gift from this catalog. It has everything from cookbooks to cookie cutters, flour, and pans. Packages of specialty flours or grains like old-fashioned graham flour, amaranth, and spelt each sell for under $5. A one-pound tin of cookies costs about $15.

Lillian Vernon, Virginia Beach, VA 23479-0002; (800) 285-5555.

This catalog carries clothes, jewelry, housewares, and children's toys—and all at reasonable prices. Though the gifts may not be the most unusual, Lillian Vernon is still a great source for standbys. Little luxuries like a silver tissue holder and mirror ($12.98), silk-covered pens from India (twelve for $9.98), personalized business card cases ($9.98), and traveling jewelry cases ($19.98) can all be ordered through the catalog. In addition, it has a wide range of goods for the home, such as a personalized door knocker ($16.98), a tool organizer ($16.98), and an adjustable wooden book rack for cookbooks ($9.98).

For children, you could buy a wood swing or wood-and-rope ladder (each sells for $19.98), a hopscotch mat ($19.98), or a set of twenty-four large cardboard bricks for building ($16.98).

Mountain Equipment Co-op, Department MCT, 1655 West Third Avenue, Vancouver, British Columbia, Canada V6J 1K1; (800) 663-2667.

Sells everything for the outdoor enthusiast, ranging from camping, hiking, and cycling equipment and clothing to books and other necessities for outdoor activities.

Pocket Songs, 50 Executive Boulevard, Elmsford, NY 10523-1325; (800) NOW-SING.

This catalog has the perfect gift for the aspiring song stylist on your list. With 1,100 tapes and CDs to choose from, it is a gold mine of presents for families, adults, and teenagers. Pocket Songs sells tapes and CDs that let you remove the vocalist from the song and become the singer. They can be used with a karaoke machine or a cassette player. On one side, the tape has the complete recording, but the vocalist can be silenced by turning down the right speaker of your sound system. The second side features the same music minus the vocalist.

Pocket Songs sells tapes with songs from over eighty years of American music, including rap, pop, showtunes, country, and gospel. Most tapes cost $12.98; exceptions are children's tapes ($10.98) and complete recordings of Broadway shows ($22.98). CDs cost $18.98. Shipping and handling are extra.

Pottery Barn, Mail-Order Department, P.O. Box 7044, San Francisco, CA 94120; (800) 922-5507.

A great source for inexpensive but trendy housewares. Miniature lanterns, votive candleholders, and sets of glasswares are all priced under $20. The Pottery Barn also sells hurricane lamps to hang out on one's patio at night, napkin rings to dress up a table, a wrought iron wine rack, and a variety of glass bottles all within your Christmas budget.

Rand McNally, Attn.: Map and Atlas Customer Service, P.O. Box 7600, Chicago, IL 60680; (800) 333-0134.

This publisher of maps and atlases is a great gift source for both adults and children. Friends planning trips would love a *Road Atlas and Travel Guide,* which includes all kinds of vacation-planning information ($18.95). Have a baseball fan on your list? *The Official Baseball Atlas* ($12.95) is a sports and travel guide that directs you through the cities and stadiums of the twenty-eight teams in the Major League. It also includes schedules for the teams' spring-training and regular seasons.

Rand McNally's books and atlases for children include *The Children's Atlas of the Environment, The Children's Atlas of Native Americans,* and *The Children's Atlas of Earth Through Time.* Each sells for $14.95.

For families that travel a lot, you could get their children a couple of Rand McNally's *Backseat Books,* travel activity books for children ages six through twelve ($6).

The Right Start Catalog, Right Start Plaza, 5334 Sterling Center Drive, Westlake Village, CA 91361-4627; (800) LITTLE-1.

This catalog will help you if you're trying to find gifts for your littlest nephews and nieces. It also sells goods that would be welcomed by any new or expectant parents on your list. Insulated tote bags for bottles ($7.95), the Right Start's Thermal Container, which comes with a lid that conceals both a fork and spoon ($9.95), and a thinsulate-lined pouch that keeps up to four bottles cold ($12.95) are great gifts for new parents on the go. Teething rings, hats, bath accessories, tapes, and videos are all available (for under $15.00 each).

Road Runner Sports, 6310 Nancy Ridge Drive, Suite 101, San Diego, CA 92121; (800) 551-5558.

Shorts, T-shirts, racing singlets, and socks are all suitable gifts for the runner, active teenager, or weekend athlete on your list. In addition to clothing, the catalog sells a number of items that would be welcomed by any athlete, like a Jogman, a carrying case for those who use walkmen ($12.99), and a Neoprene Jog Bag, which is a waterproof case for carrying a portable cassette player ($16.99). Visors ($9.99), Prem's Cool Bottle, for carrying water ($7.99), and a Solo Water Bottle, which is both a bottle and a bottle holster with compartments for your keys and cash ($22.99) are other gifts that any runner, biker, or hiker would welcome.

The catalog also carries gear for swimmers, like goggles and swim caps, and other fitness equipment, such as back supports, chin-up bars, and a Cool Sports Bandanna to keep you cool during the warm weather.

Stocking Fillas, Ltd., 133 The West Mall Department AP-1, Unit 5, Toronto, Ontario, Canada M9C 5M7; (416) 621-6100, fax (416) 621-6599.

Stocking Fillas features a wide variety of toys, games, and other playthings for children, all within your budget.

Williams-Sonoma, Mail-Order Department, P.O. Box 7456, San Francisco, CA 94120-7456; (800) 541-2233.

Another excellent source of gifts for the cooks on your list, Williams-Sonoma also sells a number of goods appropriate for families or adults who need to have their kitchenware "updated."

At Christmastime the catalog offers a wide range of cookies, gift baskets, and other food gifts that are great for families, including a kit for making gingerbread houses (about $22). It also sells useful gadgets like bottle spouts, vegetable peelers, vegetable brushes, and lobster crackers. Each of these sells for under $15 and makes a practical stocking stuffer. Dishcloths, napkins, aprons, and a wire basket that will hold two bottles ($12) are other good gift ideas.

Worldwide Games, P.O. Box 517, Colchester, CT 06415-0517; (800) 888-0987.

This catalog has gifts for any person on your list. In addition to a wide variety of puzzles and board games, Worldwide Games sells items like an automatic card shuffler ($16.95) and wooden card holders ($9.95 each). *The Backyard Games Book* ($15.95) is great for families with young children, or send a young person the catalog's Flying Penguini, three silk-screened, stuffed penguins with step-by-step juggling instructions. Worldwide Games also sells kites and favorite games like Tiddly Winks.

Gifts for Children

More than any other holiday, Christmas belongs to children. Their excitement about the holiday reminds adults how magical the season can be. When you begin buying presents for the children on your list, try to remember which were the gifts you treasured most in your childhood. While some people may tell you that a child will only be satisfied with the latest, greatest, and most expensive toy, the child could be just as pleased with a video of his or her favorite Christmas movie like *Rudolph the Red-Nosed Reindeer* or *How the Grinch Stole Christmas.* And if you promise the child a trip to the ballpark to see a pro baseball game, or a camping trip when the weather gets warmer, the gift not only would be within your budget but would provide great memories for the youngster.

If you have no idea what to get a particular child, contact the battery manufacturer Duracell's Toy Hot Line, which offers gift suggestions. The phone number is (800) BEST-TOYS. If you know what toy you want to get the child and it happens to be made by Playskool, call (800) PLAYSKL for the name of the retailer nearest you that sells Playskool toys.

Parenting magazines, *Consumer Reports,* or your local newspapers often feature articles on the best toys for kids, providing many ideas about what to get a child for Christmas.

Since finding the perfect gift for a child can be both mind

numbing and expensive, the suggestions that follow are intended to simplify your holiday shopping while keeping you within your Christmas budget.

Books, as well as books on tape, are always welcome presents. Ask librarians or grade-school teachers to recommend some of the more popular books and audiobooks.

Your post office carries beginner stamp-collectors kits for children that cost about $5. The Canada Post Corporation sells stamp kits along with coins and other products geared toward the young philatelist on your list. For more information, write to Canada Post Corporation, National Philatelic Centre, Antigonish, Nova Scotia, Canada B2G 2R8; or call (800) 565-4363.

Don't throw out your old baseball cards; they might be a welcome addition to some youngster's collection.

Old-fashioned games like Chinese checkers, chess, jacks, marbles, and dominoes are perennial favorites. Game Entertainment ($9.99), made by Capital, Inc., has equipment for playing checkers, cards, dominoes, chess, dice games, and backgammon.

Hand puppets are another good choice for young children. Folkman makes a variety of these that sell for about $13 to $16.

If the youngster likes to jump rope, get the child a rope and a book with different jump-roping rhymes. Other toys that encourage physical activity include the Woosh Flying Ring ($6.99) by Oddz on Products. And don't forget frisbees, whiffle balls and bats, and Nerf games.

For artistic youngsters, your local craft store has everything from sketchpads and coloring books to pencils, markers, and paint kits. Look for beading and macramé kits, or buy an embroidery kit for youngsters who'd like to learn needlework. The Potterycraft Clay and Paint Kit ($8.99) by Tyco Toys lets children try their hand at making pottery, from the molding of the pot to the painting of the finished product.

Budding scientists would appreciate a collection of rocks or minerals from a natural history museum. Exploratoy makes the Exploroscope ($9.99), a handheld microscope; and Uncle Milton makes the Geotek portable microscope, which sells for under $20.

117

HarperCollins Publishers sells an Environmental Detective Kit ($14.00) that contains the materials to test for acid rain or build ant farms and terrariums. The kit also comes with educational books and pamphlets that cover the various environmental problems facing our world today and suggest ways kids can help solve these problems. In Canada, a good source of gifts for young scientists is Le Naturaliste, a mail-order retailer selling products for bird watching, astronomy, and so forth. For a catalog, write to Le Naturaliste, 1990, boul. Charest o. #117, Quebec City, Quebec, Canada G1N 4K8; or call (800) 463-6848.

Games like Scattergories, Yahtzee, Monopoly, Scrabble, and Clue are great gifts not only for children or teenagers but for families as well. Keep in mind newer additions to the game world that come highly recommended from consumers groups like Parents' Choice and from children as well. Two games that are both challenging and fun are Where in the World Is Carmen San Diego? and Brain Quest. Both are made by University Games and sell for about $20. Another educational game that would be good for a child just learning to count is Snail's Pace Race ($18.95) by Ravensburger. This game teaches children about counting and colors.

A deck of cards, along with a book on how to play different games, would be a good option, as are Slinkies, yo-yos, jigsaw puzzles, and horseshoes.

A child might also appreciate a different kind of Christmas gift such as a day at the natural history museum, a sleigh ride after the first snow, or attending a local production of *A Christmas Carol*. Trips to caves, doll museums, fire engine museums, nautical or whaling museums might also pique a child's interest. You could take a child to a parade; to a flea market; to car, boat, or game trade shows as well as to local sporting events or television shows.

Take some time to search your attic before you throw out old clothes. Do you know a child who might like a box of these for dress up? Add some stories or plays the child could act out using the clothing as costumes.

A child might treasure something as simple as a kite, with plenty of string and instructions. If you live near an open space, you might invite the child over for an afternoon of kite flying. Or give the child a rubber stamp with the child's name and address on it, along with some sticks of sealing wax and a stamp with the child's initials.

You could put together a baking or sewing kit for the child. For young bakers, include a muffin pan, some premixed dried ingredients, measuring cups and spoons, and a couple of your own recipes or a book of recipes devoted to muffins. For sewers, the kit could include a precut pillow, some stuffing, and a needle and thread, or some patterns and fabric to make dolls' clothes or beanbags.

For young carpenters, put together a tool kit containing a small hammer, a little screwdriver, a tape measure, a right angle, some screws, nails, and instructions on how to make simple objects like boxes or bookends.

Check out novelty stores for trick items children can play with like pop-up snakes, dribbling water glasses, and magic kits. A good source for these kinds of gifts is the Johnson Smith *Things You Never Knew Existed* catalog. It sells the *Handbook of Magic,* along with a number of tricks children might love to learn. For a catalog, call (813) 747-2356.

Other standby gift ideas include, balls of different sizes and stuffed animals. For the girls on your list, buy bunches of hair ribbons, barrettes, and headbands.

Subscriptions to magazines are lasting Christmas presents. A year's subscription to *Boys' Life* costs about $16. For subscription information, write to Boys' Life, P.O. Box 152079, Irving, TX 75105-2079.

Consumer Reports publishes *Zillions,* which is a kind of junior Consumer Reports. Its an excellent gift for children ages eight to fourteen. A year's subscription costs $16. Write to Consumer Reports, Subscription Department, P.O. Box 51777, Boulder, CO 80321-1777.

For young sports enthusiasts, a year's subscription to *Sports*

Illustrated for Kids costs $18.95. Call (800) 633-8628. And don't forget other publications that focus on specific sports like biking or hiking or other activities a child may find interesting.

Finally, check your local library for the names of publications in the fields of science or writing that are geared toward children.

Gifts for Teenagers

Shopping for a teenager can be difficult for a couple of reasons. First, that trendy gift you bought in the fall may be out of fashion by the time Christmas rolls around. Second, in this consumer-driven society, the teenager may already have everything you'd be able to afford. Though you'd like to be able to give the teen a CD player, it just may be out of your price range this year. But don't despair, even teenagers will appreciate simpler gifts.

As with any age group, there are a number of gifts that would always be welcomed by a teenager. Since most teenagers love to listen to music, a tape or CD is a logical choice. So is a gift certificate to a music store. If you have an extensive music collection, why not tape some of your own CDs for the teenager as a gift? Or give a box of blank tapes, and let the teen decide what music to record. A book by the teenager's favorite author or on his or her favorite subject is another inexpensive yet thoughtful gift.

What is the teenager passionate about? Environmental causes? Sports? Politics? Consider a gift of a membership in a local or national club that works on causes or in fields that the teen is interested in.

Frames, posters, scrapbooks, and photo albums are other perennial favorites. An address book would also make a good gift. A journal, accompanied by the memoir of a favorite public figure or author, would be appreciated by aspiring writers.

Other gift ideas for teenagers include day trips to museums, parks, nature preserves, or trade shows; tickets to concerts, local college sporting events, plays, or lectures; and gift certificates to the local movie theater.

If the teenager is athletic, sporting or workout equipment and clothes are good options: You could give jump ropes, squash, tennis, or racquet balls, baseballs or softballs, dumbbells, T-shirts, or shorts. Also consider giving a subscription to a magazine like *Runners World, Bicycling,* or *Outdoor.* Some teens might appreciate bicycle repair kits.

For the female teens on your list, put together a box full of hair accessories like scrunchies, barrettes, combs, and clips. You could also give jars of potpourri or a certificate for a manicure. Look for small evening bags they could take to their formal dances. Check out secondhand stores for coats, scarves, hats, or jewelry, which many teens would welcome as additions to their wardrobe.

If you have a particular talent, why not offer to give the teenager a set of lessons for Christmas? Provided, of course, that he or she is interested in learning how to paint, play an instrument, or cook a certain cuisine.

Give the teen a certificate for driving lessons or a lesson in simple car repair or maintenance. If you have a video camera and the teen is a budding filmmaker, loan the camera for a couple of days of shooting.

In addition to the sports magazines mentioned earlier, the following publications would all be suitable for teenagers:

Essence
P.O. Box 53400
Boulder, CO 80322-3400
(800) 274-9395
($16 a year)

Popular Mechanics
P.O. Box 7170
Red Oak, IA 51591
(800) 333-4948
($16 a year)

Rolling Stone
Publishers Voice 150
29225 Chagrin Boulevard
Cleveland, OH 44122
(800) 568-7655
($15.97 a year)

Sassy
P.O. Box 57503
Boulder, CO 80322-7503
(800) 274-2622
($16 a year)

Seventeen
P.O. Box 55195
Boulder, CO 80322-5195
(800) 388-1749
($17 a year)

Sierra
Sierra Club
730 Polk Street
San Francisco, CA 94109
(415) 776-2211
($15 a year)

Gifts for Adults

Adults can often be the most difficult people on your list to buy for, in part because they seem to have everything, but also because they may be reluctant to give you a "wish list" of what they'd like for Christmas. Although many practical gifts might be out of your price range, there are a lot of items out there for under $20 that would make their lives a little easier.

If you're unsure what to buy a certain adult on your list, look around that person's home on your next visit. And when he or she is rummaging around the kitchen or garage for some gadget or utensil, keep your ears open for a remark like, "Oh, I need to buy one." Also keep in mind the interests, hobbies, or avocations of the individual. What type of music does this person listen to? What's his or her favorite cuisine? By narrowing your focus it will be easier for you to decide what to buy.

Some little things that make great gifts include soaps, a nice pen, and a spill-free coffee mug for the car. Throw in some special coffees with the mug for a more substantial gift.

Ideas for those on your list who drive a lot: books on tape, maps, change holders for tolls, a rack for audiocassettes or CDs, and a tire repair kit.

For the frequent flyers on your list, you can purchase a few inexpensive items that might make their travel time less stressful. These include a travel iron, clothesline, or folding hangers. Those who go abroad would appreciate books on the cities they're visiting, tip purses filled with different currencies, or phrase books.

A long plane ride might be a lot more comfortable if the passenger has an inflatable neck rest or pillow, eye shades, or a couple of favorite tapes to play on his or her Walkman.

Checkbook holders and purses for small change or tokens are great for daily outings. Keep in mind key rings, credit-card holders, and tote bags as well.

Campers on your list might like a little luxury in their lives when they're spending a night under the stars. GSI Outdoors sells a mini espresso maker for $15. For more information, call (619) 271-7816. On cold nights, they'd appreciate a pair of Feet Heaters; these fleece socks will keep a person warm even when they're wet. They're made by Wyoming Woolens and sell for $11 to $15. Call (800) 732-2991.

For $15, you can enroll any person over the age of fifty as a member of the American Association of Retired Persons (AARP). Members get discounts on a number of goods and services. Write to AARP Membership Processing Center, P.O. Box 199, Long Beach, CA 90848-9983; or call (202) 434-2277.

If the adults on your list have other special interests or hobbies, a membership in a local or national club is a good gift idea. Your local library has a reference book entitled *Encyclopedia of Associations* that lists special-interest organizations by subject.

Gardeners on your list might appreciate a variety of bulbs or seeds from your local nursery. Look for gardening gloves or special tools they might need. A gift of waterproof plant markers would help them keep track of the perennials in their garden. Gardener's Supply, a direct-mail retailer, sells a set of twenty-five of these for $10.95. Call (802) 863-1700.

Prints or old maps from thrift shops, rummage sales, or local museums make great gifts. If you're in Washington D.C., check out the National Archives for its wealth of reproduction drawings, engravings, photographs, and old documents dealing with every facet of U.S. history and life. Framed, these make lovely presents. Purdham, a Canadian mail-order retailer, sells a wide variety of reproductions of maps and historical documents. In addition, it sells replicas of antique cars and trains, which could be a great gift for a friend who's an avid collector. For a catalog, write to Purdham, 3039 du Portage, Carignan, Quebec, Canada J3L 2B8. Canadian residents should include a self-addressed stamped envelope; from the United States, add a $2 check for postage and handling.

Letter writers on your list would appreciate more stationery, a clipboard, or a box containing pens, pencils, stamps, and airmail stickers. Address labels, a rubber address stamp and ink pad, postcards, correspondence cards, or an address book would all be welcome gifts.

For the cooks on your list, cookbooks are a sure choice. Give books on different cuisines, and make each gift that much more special by including some of the special and unusual spices these recipes call for. You could also buy the cook pots of fresh herbs and include directions on how to dry them and recipes the herbs are used in. If you have a group of friends who are avid cooks, why not get together and exchange five of your favorite recipes as Christmas gifts? Each friend would buy a recipe box, place five recipes in it, and present it to another member of the group. In addition, they'd provide copies of the recipes for all the other members of the group. The recipe box would then be filled by the recipes each person receives from his or her group of friends.

Put together coffee and tea samplers for your relatives. You can buy both in bulk and put them in jars and containers you've collected throughout the year. Label each container with a description of the coffee or tea, and place the samples in a wooden box or tray.

Young adults who've just moved into their first apartment probably need a number of things to make their kitchen functional. Give them a book of your recipes or a couple of good basic cookbooks. Heavy-duty can or bottle openers, knives, and cutting boards are all useful. You could also make a little toolbox for them; fill it with nails, picture hooks, a hammer, and a screwdriver.

Some kitchen appliances are not as expensive as you might think. Black and Decker sells a Handy Juicer for about $19, and Hamilton Beach has blenders ranging in price from $20 to $25. Two reasonably priced mixers are the Moulinex Max-Chopper (about $25) and the Black and Decker HC20 (about $20). If you want to go in on a gift with another friend, why not buy a Crockpot for around $30?

Buy a bunch of big mason jars, and fill them with different kinds of pasta, candies, nuts or sunflower seeds, or something you made yourself like apple butter, jellies, or different sauces. By doing this, you can finish off a lot of your Christmas shopping with a single trip to the grocery store and an afternoon at home preparing the goods.

Like the children and teenagers on your list, the adults would enjoy a subscription to a magazine. Many people are becoming more concerned about saving money for retirement or for their children's college education. They might appreciate a subscription to a magazine like *Kiplinger's Personal Finance Magazine* or *Money*. You could also buy them a ledger that would help them keep track of their savings, investments, and taxes.

Gifts for Families

You can be a bit more creative with family gifts. Many times a present to a group of people can be something you made yourself, like a big batch of cookies in a tin or a special Christmas basket filled with ornaments and food. For family gifts, there are always such standbys as coffee-table books, videos, and games, which everyone can enjoy. Consider indoor games like Risk, backgammon, checkers, or puzzles; and outdoor games like badminton, horseshoes, or a volleyball net and ball. Holiday-related items, like a Christmas tablecloth, a set of Christmas coffee mugs, or a set of holiday glasses are other safe bets.

Gifts for the home such as personalized stationery with the family's address on it or welcome mats for the front door would be appreciated. For people with patios and pools, purchase items they can use when the weather is warm. Small plastic tables, plastic tumblers or serving trays, citronella candles are perfect for use outside. Rafts, floating games, and inflatable balls to toss around can all be used in the pool.

Throughout the year, keep your eye out for wicker baskets that are on sale. Fill little ones with bulbs of garlic or packages of fresh herbs for the family's kitchen, or in bigger baskets put dishtowels or soaps for the family's bathroom.

Families who travel a good deal and have a newborn would appreciate a baby traveling kit. Include a plastic-lined bag with disposable diapers, a bottle warmer, formula, baby toy, towelettes, a teething ring, spoon, and a jar or two of baby food.

You can also give families subscriptions to a magazine, like *National Geographic, Consumer Reports, Yankee Magazine, Readers Digest,* or one of the many publications that focuses on the city they live in (e.g., *New York, Philadelphia, Chicago, Toronto Life*).

If you're putting together a gift for your own family, tape some of your relatives talking about their favorite Christmas. Include stories from both the older and younger family members. You could also videotape them or have them dictate their stories to you. Send copies of the tapes or transcripts to all your aunts and uncles as a Christmas present. Doing something like this creates some cherished and lasting memories for your family.

Gifts for the Vision Impaired

There are a number of places from which you can order Christmas gifts for the vision impaired. First and foremost would be Books on Tape, which carries a large selection of audio books. Write to Books on Tape, P.O. Box 7900, Newport Beach, CA 92660; or call (800) 252-6996.

G. K. Hall and Co. has a catalog featuring Large Print Books. For a copy, write to Large Print Books, 70 Lincoln Street, Boston, MA 02111; or call (800) 257-5755.

The American Printing House for the Blind sells braille books. Write to the American Printing House for the Blind, P.O. Box 6085, Louisville, KY 40206; or call (800) 223-1839.

Lastly, the *New York Times* prints a weekly, large-type newspaper. A six-month subscription costs $35.10. To order write to the *New York Times*, Mail Subscriptions, P.O. Box 9564, Uniondale, NY 11556-9564 or call (800) 631-2580.

Along the same lines, why not "do it yourself" and make your own tape of a book and present it as a gift to someone you know who is vision impaired?

From Your Own Workshop: Gifts You Make Yourself

One of the nicest ways you can say "Merry Christmas" to the people on your list is to make something yourself. If you're artistic, you can paint a favorite scene for the special person on your list or draw a picture of his or her house. Those who embroider or do needlepoint can create personalized pillows or frame some of their needlework as a gift. Knitters can make Christmas stockings, hats, mittens, or scarves as time allows.

Even if you don't have any special talents, or if you find yourself running out of time, you can still make gifts of food. Maybe you have a special recipe for Christmas cookies that's been handed down through the generations. If so, make up a batch and give them to your friends along with a copy of the recipe. Or you might want to prepare a variety of foods and put them in a little basket with an ornament hanging from the handle.

The following are favorite recipes from my family and friends for toppings, cookies, and other foods that are perfect for a Christmas basket. Why not try them out? Sometime early in the holiday season, devote one day to shopping and baking, and put together baskets of Christmas cheer for your family and friends.

MISSING CHOCOLATE SQUARE COOKIES

A favorite of the Gilbert family of Philadelphia, this recipe was missing from the family archives for some time until it was redis-covered a few years ago. These squares are a great treat for the chocolate lovers on your list.

17 unsugared graham crackers crumbled
⅔ cup broken walnuts
1 cup condensed milk
16-ounce package of chocolate chips

Crumble all the ingredients together and mix. Spread mixture into a well-greased 8- × -8-inch pan. Bake at 350° F for 20 minutes. Cut into squares.

DIANE'S SPECIAL SYRUPS

These delicious toppings, served over ice cream or sponge cakes, are a perfect way to end a festive holiday dinner.

Use any combination of:
Strawberries and rum
Cherries and brandy
Raspberries and cognac

First make a sugar syrup by combining 1 cup of sugar and 1 cup of water. Heat the mixture to 230°F.

Then add the liquor of choice, mixing one part liquor with one part syrup. Pour this liquid over the fruit, which has been packed into clean glass jars. Seal and store in a cool place for two months. Refrigerate the sauces once they've been opened.

A couple of tips when making these sauces: Run the glasses through the dishwasher before you pack them with fruit, and make sure the fruit is clean.

MAB'S PEPPER JELLY

For many years, Mary Anne Burns, or Mab, has been making her pepper jelly at Christmastime for her group of friends. Served on crackers covered with cream cheese, this red or green jelly makes a delightful holiday hors d'oeuvre.

½ cup jalapeno peppers, seeded and ground
¾ cup bell or red peppers, seeded and ground

6½ cups sugar
1½ cups apple cider vinegar
1 6-ounce package of Certo pectin
Red or green food coloring (only two to three
drops)
8 ½-pint sterile jelly glasses

Combine peppers, sugar, vinegar, and bring to a hard boil, stirring constantly. Add pectin and food coloring, and bring to a second, hard, rolling boil. Boil for 1 minute. Remove and let stand for 5 minutes. Skim the foam off the top, being careful not to remove the peppers. Fill jelly glasses to within ⅛ to ¼ inch from the top. Seal and place upside down for 5 minutes. Check the seal in 1 hour to make sure the "pop" is down. Serve the jelly with cream cheese and crackers.

ENGLISH TEA CAKES

The smell of these English Tea Cakes warming in the oven will get any weary adult out of bed on Christmas morning. This treat is a festive way to start the holiday when served with a big cup of hot coffee, cocoa, or tea.

3 eggs
1 cup sugar
1 cup melted butter
3 yeast cakes dissolved in 2 cups lukewarm
  water
½ pound golden raisins
4 tablespoons orange peel
1 teaspoon salt
1 teaspoon nutmeg
10 cups of sifted flour

Combine these ingredients, and let the dough rise. Knead the dough, split it evenly, put it in two greased 9-inch round pans, and let it rise again. Spread the dough in each pan, and bake at 375°F for 10 minutes. Let the cakes cool, then remove them from the pans. Split them horizontally. Put the bottom of each back in its pan and spread with the following, creamed together:

¾ pound butter
1 pound confectioners' sugar

Place the top back on each cake, and bake at 300°F for 25 minutes. Cut each cake into eight pieces, and serve warm.

HERB VINEGAR /GARLIC VINEGAR

These vinegars are lovely additions to any Christmas basket. Tie a bright red ribbon about the necks of the bottles, and include a recipe that might call for one of the vinegars.

To prepare herb vinegar: Save wine or other narrow-necked bottles and their corks. Scrub the corks clean, or use plastic-topped bottles that have been run through the dishwasher. Place 1 cup of a slightly crushed fresh herb, either tarragon, basil, dill, rosemary, parsley, or thyme, in a quart mason jar. Bring a quart of white or red wine vinegar to a boil, and pour it into the mason jar, over the herb. Cap this mixture, and let it steep for two weeks. Then strain the liquid into the bottles, and put a fresh sprig of the herb in each and seal the bottle. If you cork the bottles, rather than using the plastic tops, dip the corks and the tops of the bottles in melted sealing or candle wax.

To make garlic vinegar: Put some cloves of garlic on a bamboo skewer, put the skewer and a quart of white or red vinegar in a mason jar, and let the liquid steep for two weeks. When making garlic vinegar, remember you don't need to heat the vinegar. After two weeks, strain the vinegar, seal, and label.

BOURBON BALLS

These delicious, no-bake cookies are a welcome treat at Christmastime. Easy to make, they are a must for any bag of goodies you put together.

3 cups vanilla wafer crumbs (12-oz pkg.)
1 cup chopped pecans
3 tablespoons light corn syrup
½ cup bourbon
½ cup cocoa
A pinch of salt
2 cups confectioners' sugar

Roll wafers to a fine crumb, or run through a food processor. Blend thoroughly crumbs, nuts, corn syrup, cocoa, bourbon, salt, and 1 cup of the confectioners' sugar. Form into balls, and roll each one twice in the remaining confectioners' sugar.

CANDY-STRIPE TWISTS

These cookies are a holiday favorite. Leave them straight, or bend the ends so they look like candy canes.

3¼ cups flour
1 egg

4 teaspoons baking powder
½ teaspoon oil of anise
1 teaspoon salt
¼ cup milk
½ cup butter or margarine
1¼ cups sugar
Red food coloring

Sift together flour, baking powder, and salt. In a separate bowl cream together butter and sugar, then beat in the egg and the oil of anise. Add the dry ingredients to the creamed mixture, one-third at a time, alternating the dry ingredients with the milk. Blend well.

Once the ingredients are blended, split the dough in half and tint one half with red food coloring. Leave the other half plain. Pinch off about a teaspoon of both the red and plain dough, and roll each until it is pencil thin and about 5 inches long. Place the ends of each of the strips together, and twist into a rope. Bake the twists on an ungreased cookie sheet at 350°F for about 10 minutes, or until they are firm. Do not brown the twists on top.

CRESCENT COOKIES

These cookies are a favorite of the Kahr family, who make them only at Christmastime at their home in Newton, Massachusetts. It's worth waiting a whole year to taste them.

½ pound butter or margarine
2 cups chopped pecans
½ cup sugar
1 teaspoon vanilla
2 cups flour
3 teaspoons water

Cream together butter and sugar. Add flour, chopped nuts, and vanilla. Mix well. Add water, and mix until the mixture no longer clings to the sides of the bowl. Shape the dough into crescents. Bake the cookies on an ungreased cookie sheet at 350°F for 12 to 15 minutes. Do not let the cookies brown. Sprinkle them in confectioners' sugar while they are still warm.

🌿 GLAZED LIME NUT BREAD 🌿

The following is a tasty change from the more traditional tea breads made with blueberries, poppyseeds, or cranberries.

¼ pound butter
1 cup plus 2 tablespoons sugar
2 eggs
Grated peel from one lime
Juice from one lime
2 cups sifted all-purpose flour
2½ teaspoons baking powder
1 teaspoon salt
¾ cup milk
½ cup chopped walnuts
2 tablespoons sugar

Cream together butter and 1 cup of the sugar until light and fluffy. Add eggs and lime peel and beat well. Next, add all but 2 teaspoons of the lime juice and mix well.

Sift together flour, baking powder, and salt, then add this to the creamed mixture, alternating with the milk. After each addition, beat the mixture until it's smooth. Stir in walnuts, and pour into a greased loaf pan measuring 9 × 5 × 2½ inches.

Bake at 350°F for 50 to 55 minutes. Cool in the pan for about 10 minutes, then spoon the mixture of the two remaining 2 teaspoons of lime juice and 2 tablespoons of sugar over the top. Remove from the pan and cool.

🍃 LIME GINGER COOKIES 🍃

One can never have enough recipes for great-tasting cookies. The following is one the Caton family likes to use during the holidays, when they celebrate a Cape Cod Christmas at their home in West Barnstable, Massachusetts.

2 cups sifted flour
2 teaspoons baking powder
½ teaspoon salt (optional)

¼ teaspoon ginger
1 cup butter or butter-flavored Crisco
1¼ cups sugar
2 eggs
3 teaspoons lime zest
4 teaspoons lime juice

Sift together flour, baking powder, salt, and ginger. Cream together butter and sugar. Add eggs, lime zest, lime juice, and blend with dry ingredients. Refrigerate for a couple of hours.

When you bake these cookies, take out only enough dough for each cookie sheet; otherwise the dough will get too soft from being left out too long.

Drop level tablespoons or full teaspoons of the dough on an ungreased baking sheet. Press the dough down with a fork. Bake the cookies at 350° F for 10 to 12 minutes, or until they are lightly browned around the edges. Remove and cool on wire racks.

These cookies freeze very well. Frozen cookies should be taken out of the freezer and allowed to defrost for about 20 minutes to half an hour before serving. If you put them in a toaster oven at 275° F for about 8 minutes or so, the cookies will taste as though they were just baked.

AGNES ALEXANDER'S OATMEAL COOKIES

Agnes Alexander's original recipe called for a half pound of lard. It was created at a time when people cooked with lard instead of shortening. Although the results were delicious, in light of our new health consciousness, the lard has been exchanged for shortening or Crisco.

1 cup shortening or butter-flavored Crisco
1 cup brown sugar
2 cups oatmeal
2 cups flour
1 teaspoon baking soda in ¼ cup of water
½ teaspoon salt (optional)

151

2 teaspoons vanilla
2 or 3 tablespoons milk
1 heaping cup chopped nuts

Mix all the ingredients together. Drop heaping teaspoons of the dough on a greased cookie sheet, and press the dough down with a fork. Bake the cookies at 350°F to 375°F for 12 to 15 minutes. Remove and let cool.

Simply Christmas has presented a number of suggestions for celebrating the holidays in new or old-fashioned ways. Christmas is such a wonderful time of the year, it's a shame to lose sight of its message of love, hope, and friendship in all the rush that surrounds it. So try to take a different approach to the holiday this year: Keep it simple, emphasize tradition, and do one thing—whether it's through a gift you buy or an event you attend—that will in some way help others who may not have the means to celebrate the holiday season.

INDEX

153